RAMBLE
LEEDS

Volume 2 : West of Leeds

24 MOSTLY CIRCULAR WALKS WITH SKETCH MAPS

Compiled by

Douglas Cossar

for the Ramblers' Association (West Riding Area)

Other publications by the Ramblers' Association (West Riding Area)

Kiddiwalks (new edition, Spring 1995*)*
Douglas Cossar, *The Airedale Way* (1996*)*
Douglas Cossar, *Ramblers' Wakefield* (1997*)*
Marje Wilson, *The Brontë Way* (1997)
Dales Way Handbook (with the Dales Way Association, annually)
Douglas Cossar, *Ramblers' Bradford*, volume 1 (1999)
Douglas Cossar, *Ramblers' Leeds*, volume 1 East of Leeds (1999)

Ramblers' Leeds first published 1995
2nd revised and expanded edition in two volumes 1999/2000

© Douglas Cossar 1995, 2000

RAMBLERS' ASSOCIATION (WEST RIDING AREA)
27 Cookridge Avenue, Leeds LS16 7NA

ISBN 1 901184 24 2

Front cover photographs: Hunger Hills, Horsforth, on the Leeds Country Way (Walk 11), Kirkstall Abbey (Walk 22), Calverley Bridge (Walk 10), milestone at Bramhope (Walk 19). *Rear cover photographs*: Bramhope Cross (Walk 18), Golden Acre (Walk 20), stile above Hawksworth village (Walk 15).

Publishers' Note
At the time of publication all footpaths used in these walks were designated as public rights of way or permissive footpaths, but it should be borne in mind that diversion orders may be made from time to time. Although every care has been taken in the preparation of this guide, neither the author nor the publisher can accept responsibility for those who stray from the routes described.

This one for

Colin and Fleur

in recognition of many years of
inspiration and friendship

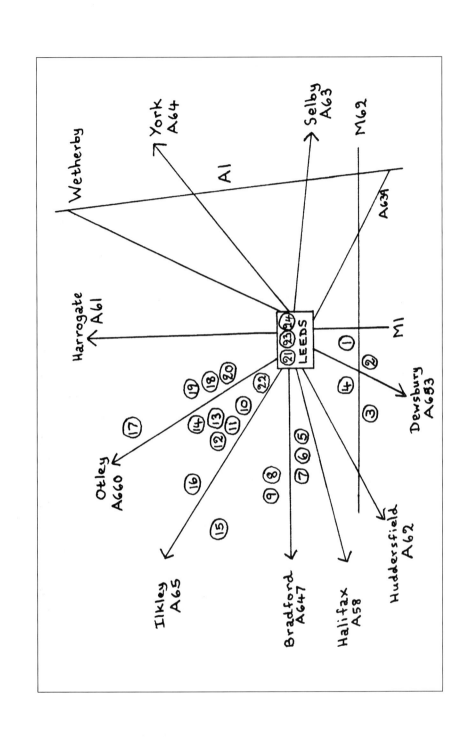

Contents

The **Ramblers' Association**, a registered charity, is an organisation dedicated to the preservation and care of the countryside and its network of footpaths, and to helping people to appreciate and enjoy them.

Through its Central Office the Ramblers' Association lobbies and campaigns for more effective legislation to achieve

- the preservation and improvement of the footpath network

- better access to the countryside

- the preservation and enhancement for the benefit of the public of the beauty of the countryside.

Since its formation in 1935 the Ramblers' Association has grown into a powerful campaigning organisation with a membership of 125,000.

The Association relies on many volunteers working at Area and Local Group level to help achieve these objectives.

The **West Riding Area** is one of the 51 Areas of the Ramblers' Association which cover England, Wales and Scotland. It includes the whole of West Yorkshire and parts of North Yorkshire around Selby, York, Harrogate, Ripon, Skipton and Settle, as well as the southern part of the Yorkshire Dales National Park. The Area has over 4,000 members and is divided into 13 Local Groups.

The **Local Groups** carry out the work of the Ramblers' Association by keeping an eye on the state of footpaths in their area and monitoring proposed closures and diversions.

- They put pressure on their Local Authority to take action to remove obstructions and re-instate footpaths after ploughing.

- They do practical work of footpath clearance and waymarking, and can erect stiles and footbridges.

- Where the Local Authority has set up consultation procedures, e.g. Footpath Forums, the Local Group will normally send a representative.

- Many Local Groups produce their own programme of walks.

Regular walks are a very important part of Ramblers' activities. As well as ensuring that local footpaths are used, they provide healthy recreation and the opportunity to make new friends.

If you use and enjoy the footpath network, please help us to protect it, by joining the Ramblers' Association. For further information write to the West Riding Area Membership Secretary

Mrs Dora Tattersall, 2 Southend, Raines Road, Giggleswick, Settle BD24 0BW, or to

The Ramblers' Association, 2nd Floor, Camelford House, 87-90 Albert Embankment, London SE1 7TW.

Author's note.

Volume 1 of this second edition of *Ramblers' Leeds*, covering roughly the area east of Leeds, which appeared in 1999, contained walks 1-20 of the first edition, plus five new walks. The walks in this second volume reflect much less closely those in the earlier edition. I have used only 10 walks from the previous book, and they have been fully revised, 2 more are based mainly on those in the earlier book, 3 more have been adapted from walks in the earlier book, and 9 are completely new.

There are various reasons for this. Since *Ramblers' Leeds* first appeared in the spring of 1995 my *Ramblers' Wakefield* and *Ramblers' Bradford* have been published, and whereas in the first *Ramblers' Leeds* I strayed into neighbouring districts quite frequently, in this new edition I have tried to stay within the Leeds District, although I have not been totally successful! In addition, I have discovered more paths which I felt were worth including, and I wanted to fill up one or two gaps left by the earlier book. So there has been considerable recasting of the walks, and I hope this has resulted in improvements.

I have tried to achieve a wide geographical spread of walks, and I hope that on the whole the two parts of *Ramblers' Leeds* represent reasonably well the variety and interest of the landscapes of Leeds. Those of us who live in and around the city have much to be grateful for.

All the paths used are definitive rights of way or permissive footpaths, and they are on the whole in good shape, thanks both to the vigilance and pressure of the Ramblers' Association and to the committed attitude of Leeds Leisure Services Public Rights of Way Section. If you should encounter any obstacles, obstructions, nuisances or other difficulties, please report them, either to the Footpaths Officer of the Leeds Group of the RA, Alan Beal, 433 Oakwood Lane, Leeds LS8 3LF (Tel.:0113-240-2615), or to Leeds City Council's Rights of Way Section at the Red Hall Estate, Wetherby Road, Leeds LS17 8NB (Tel: 0113-232-9422). As a result of recent tragic accidents, dogs now seem generally to be kept under much better control than formerly, but do look out for bulls at large in pastures in the summer months, and take suitable evasive action, even if this means a minor trespass. Better safe than sorry!

I am again most grateful to Roger Brookes of the Rights of Way Section for giving me his time and the benefit of his knowledge of local footpath developments and for suggesting corrections and improvements to my routes. The final responsibility for the walks is of course my own.

All the walks can be located on the Ordnance Survey Landranger map 104 (Leeds & Bradford, Harrogate & Ilkley, scale 1:50 000), and at the start of each walk I have given details of the relevant Explorer sheet(s), which have now replaced the Pathfinder Series (scale 1:25 000). All the walks in this volume can be found on three Explorer maps: 289 Leeds, 288 Bradford & Huddersfield and 297 (formerly 27) Lower Wharfedale. The sketch maps which accompany each walk are based on these Explorer maps and are reproduced with the permission of the Controller of H.M.S.O. They are intended to give an overview of the walk and to supplement the description, but as they are greatly simplified, particularly in built-up areas, **they should not be used as a substitute for the description**. Please read the descriptions carefully: I have tried to make them clear and unambiguous and to eliminate the risk of misinterpretation. But in my experience lots of people go astray through not concentrating on the text of a walk, inadvertently skipping a line or jumping by mistake from one stile to the next, or just losing the place through being engrossed in conversation with their companions!

All the walks are accessible by public transport, and I have given details as they are known to me at the moment. But please do check this information with West Yorkshire Metro (Tel: 0113-245-7676).

The photographs of Hunger Hills and the stile above Hawksworth (cover), the stile near Lineham Farm (Walk 20) and Woodkirk Church (Walk 3) were taken by Roger Brookes and are © Leeds City Council; I am grateful to Roger for permission to use them. I took the rest of the photographs myself.

I should like to dedicate this volume to Colin and Fleur Speakman. When I first joined the Ramblers' Association almost thirty years ago, Colin was Secretary of the West Riding Area, and it was to him and his books that I owed my first acquaintance with local footpaths. His knowledge of Yorkshire history and footpaths is vast, as his many publications testify, his energy and organising ability quite exceptional, and his commitment, with Fleur, to the preservation of all that is best in the West Riding and the Yorkshire Dales total. I am proud to count them among my friends.

Douglas Cossar,
August 2000

Remember the Country Code:
Guard against all risk of fire.
Take your litter home. As well as being unsightly, it may be a hazard to livestock.
If you find a gate closed, be careful to close it again behind you. If it is open, leave it open.
Do not pollute streams or rivers, ponds, lakes or reservoirs.
Keep dogs under control: they may frighten other walkers or be a threat to livestock.
Protect, wildlife, plants and trees.
Keep to public paths across farmland.
Take special care on country roads.
Use gates and stiles to cross fences, hedges and walls.
Make no unnecessary noise.
Leave livestock, crops and machinery alone.
Enjoy the countryside and respect its life and work.

MIDDLETON PARK TO THORPE ON THE HILL

WALK 1

5¾ miles (9¼ km); Explorer 289. Woodland walking in Middleton Park is followed by a ridge with fine views (part of the South Leeds Heritage Trail), and the return is on pleasant field paths.

By bus: 74/74A/74B/75/76 Moor Grange/Horsforth-City Centre (Headrow)-Middleton (frequent service, evenings and Sundays half-hourly) to the entrance to Middleton Park on Town Street, Middleton. Enter the Park through the main gate and fork right down a tarmac drive.

By car: Enter Middleton Park through the main entrance on Town Street, Middleton and immediately fork right to drive down to a large car park on the left. Return to the tarmac drive and turn left down it.

Pass the Lakeside Centre (a small modern building behind iron railings) and a large old building which used to be the café, pass round a large metal barrier and at a crossing of tracks turn left. Enter the woods and continue on the broad track. At a fork you can go either way, because the paths soon meet up again. You are joined by a broad track coming down from the pond on the left. At the next fork keep left: Middleton golf course is now to your left. At the next fork again keep left, ignoring a narrow path further left, closer to the golf course. A little further on ignore another narrow path forking left, and at the next major fork keep right, in a few yards joining a broad tarmac drive: turn left along it.

When you reach a major fork, keep right on a descending tarmac path which in a few yards passes an iron bollard. In 100 yards ignore a broad unsurfaced track forking right, cross over a cross path (on the left there is a flight of steps), pass between some chunks of concrete, and at the next major junction cross straight over the broad track to follow a narrower footpath opposite, which in a yard or two bends slightly left and becomes paved. Follow this narrow hedged path to where it ends at a broader tarmac path and keep forward along this. Cross straight over the Beeston Ring Road and go down Bodmin Road opposite. Follow it as it bends left, and just before an open grassy area on the right, turn right through a barrier (there is an information board about the South Leeds Heritage Trail) and follow the broad track.

Stay with the track as it bends right, and when it forks, keep left. After a time there is a good view right to Morley. Stay with this well-made path, partly through woodland, partly with open views, keeping right at two major forks, until it climbs steeply to a T-junction. Turn right (after admiring the view) and follow the path to where it ends at the A654. Turn left along the footway. Cross over Thorpe Garth, then cross

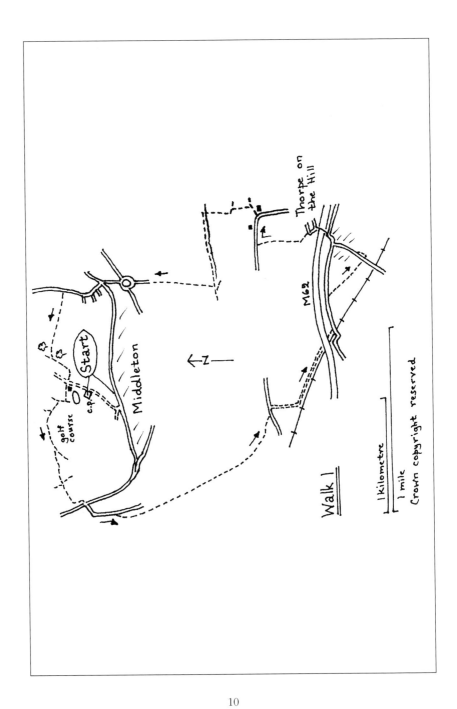

Walk 1

1 kilometre
1 mile
Crown copyright reserved

10

the main road and take the signposted bridleway opposite. This is a track which goes down through a varied assortment of buildings, "furniture" and livestock. At the bottom turn left along a track parallel to the railway.

Pass under the M62, keeping to a fenced footpath on the left of the track, and follow this to a kissing-gate and a motor road. Turn left along the footway. Just after the first street light on the **opposite** side of the road, cross the road and take the narrow path forking right and crossing a barrier. After about 80 yards keep right at a fork along the slightly less distinct path. Follow this path through what feels like quite remote countryside until it passes through a tunnel under a road. On the far side turn left up the tarmac track, and on reaching the road, keep forward along the footway through Thorpe on the Hill.

Shortly after the main road bends right, fork left off it along a tarmac footpath which leads to a covered footbridge over the M62. On the far side fork left up the street which passes to the left of Thorpe School. Where the road bends right, fork left along a short length of fenced footpath into a field, and turn right round the field edge. Keep along the edge of the field to the next road. Cross and turn right along the footway. When the road bends right, fork left through a gap in the wall and keeping the farm buildings on your right walk forward along a track. Where the track forks, keep left, and follow it to pass between two strips of woodland.

Keep forward over the next field. On the far side descend by broad steps to cross Throstle Carr Beck by a bridge and turn left along the track, shortly passing through a metal barrier. Follow the track parallel to the beck, invisible to your left, until you reach another metal barrier. Immediately after this turn sharp right, where there should be a clear path over the large field. Aim for the corner of an old field boundary projecting into the field, and from it continue up to a gap in the hedge at the top. (This path may be affected by proposed housing development.) Now keep forward with a hedge on the left and follow it to a high wire factory fence. Bear left along it, to reach a road at a bus turning circle.

Keep forward along the road, pass the bus shelters, and walk clockwise round the large roundabout, crossing the Beeston Ring Road and going down the next road (Sharp Lane). On reaching the next major road (Town Street) cross straight over and go down Newhall Road opposite. When the footway ends, keep forward along the grass verge until you reach a clear footpath leaving at an acute angle on the left with a fence to its right. Follow this fence all the way to Middleton Wood.

Enter the woods and in a few yards keep left at a junction of paths. When you reach a broad path, keep left along it. At the next large path junction bear right with the broad track, and when you reach a broad tarmac drive, turn left along it to return to the start of the walk.

EAST AND WEST ARDSLEY

WALK 2

5¾ miles (9¼ km); Explorer 289; an easy, remarkably "green" walk in what is a fairly built-up area on the southern fringe of the Leeds District.

By bus: No. 117/118 Leeds-Wakefield (half hourly, hourly evenings and Sundays) to the first stop in the Wakefield Road (A650) after the enormous Tingley roundabout. The walk starts at Tingley Post Office.
By car: From Leeds take the A653 Dewsbury road as far as the enormous Tingley roundabout, where it crosses the M62, and there turn left into the Wakefield Road (A650). In a short distance you pass Tingley Post Office, where the walk starts, but keep on until you reach the A654 on the left, signposted Rothwell and Middleton. Drive down it, but just before it crosses the motorway turn left along Thorpe Lane. Shortly after the houses start the road widens and there is room to park on the right hand side. Walk to the far end of Thorpe Lane, where a tarmac footpath returns you to the A650. Walk along to Tingley Post Office.

At Tingley Post Office cross the main road and turn left. In a small patch of grass is the war memorial. Immediately after this turn half right and cross the side road to a tarmac footpath opposite. On reaching the housing estate keep straight forward, crossing the street where it bends slightly right and keeping forward along the tarmac footway. At the next cross street turn left for a few yards, then cross the street and pass through the barrier into a tarmac footpath. Keep right at a fork, then keep straight down, ignoring paths forking left and right, until at the final fork keep left, pass through a barrier, ignore a street on the right and at the next junction of paths turn right. On reaching Westerton Road, cross it and turn right.

A signposted footpath leads to the left of the British Oak pub. Enter the field and walk down its right hand edge. At the end of the field drop down the bank and climb the other side to a fence corner. Turn right, to follow a clear path between the fence on your left and a wood on the right. Where the fence begins to curve left, leave it and take the path straight ahead, and when you reach a field, bear right along its right hand edge. You are now on Beggarington Hill. The tower of Woodkirk Church is visible to the right. Soon you have houses to the left. The path becomes a track and then a tarmac lane which leads to the Wakefield-Batley road. In the distance is the spire of Ossett Church. Cross the road and turn right. On the corner here is West Ardsley Post Office.

Pass the Hare & Hounds, and opposite the road to Morley (Baghill Road) turn left along Hey Beck Lane. You have now joined the Leeds Country Way. At the last house fork right down a grassy track. Don't cross the bridge over Hey Beck into the farmyard at the bottom, but immediately before it turn left along a path which soon reaches a stile into a field, and walk along the right hand edge of this. When the fence on your right turns right, keep straight forward, cutting the corner of the

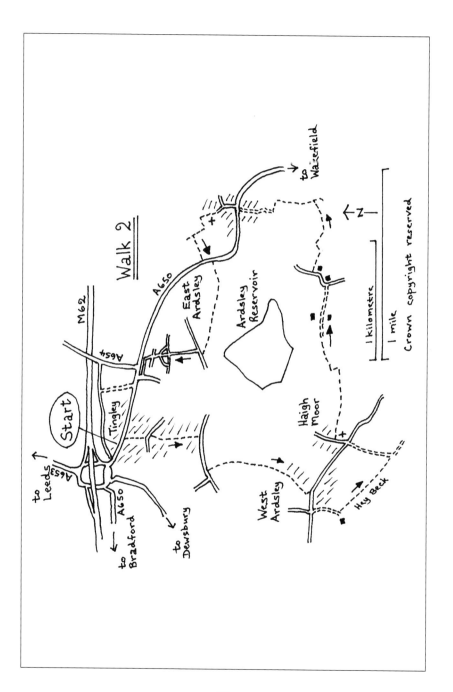

Walk 2

13

field, to a redundant stile, then keep along to the left of the trees and you will soon see the next stile ahead, where a hedge coming down from the left meets a fence by some tall trees. Keep straight across the next large field: the next stile is in the far right hand corner just in front of a small redbrick building. Cross the stile and turn left up the track, here leaving the Leeds Country Way.

When you reach the main road at Haigh Moor cross over and walk up Haigh Moor Road opposite. About 30 yards past the Methodist Church turn right along the signposted track. When this bears left, cross the stile ahead and walk along the left hand edge of two fields. Cross the stile in the next field corner, cross over a track and continue forward into an old hedged footpath. At the far end of the field keep forward: the path drops then bears left, before turning right over a footbridge to a stile. Walk up the right hand edge of the field, cross a sort of terrace and another stile, then continue up the right hand edge of the next field. Ardsley Reservoir is over to your left. Cross the next stile to the right of two large gates and follow the lane forward to the next motor road. There is a view half right to Wakefield city centre.

Cross the road and turn left along it. Soon it bears left and on the right are imposing iron gates into a modern house. A few yards further on is a signposted footpath on the right. Walk down the few steps and along the fenced path. Where it ends, keep straight forward across the field to a track. Go right along the track for about 25 yards. The right of way turns left over the field here to a marker post on the far side, but most walkers keep along the track. If you do cross the field, when you reach the marker post turn right down the edge of the field, to rejoin the track: turn left through the large double gates and follow the fence on your left to a stile. Cross it and keep forward with a hedge to your left; when the hedge ends, keep straight forward across the field to a stile in the fence on the far side just to the left of some trees.

Do not cross the stile, but turn left, keeping the fence on your right. In the top corner ignore the stile on the right but cross the one ahead and continue uphill with the fence/hedge on your right. Cross a stile into an enclosed footpath, which after a time bears right as a track. When you reach houses, keep forward to the A650. Cross it and turn right for a few yards, then left up Cherry Tree Walk. When the road forks, keep forward along a tarmac footpath, and at the top keep straight on with the churchyard wall of St.Michael's East Ardsley on your left. At the far end go through a small gate and turn left, still with the churchyard on your left. The wall is replaced by a fence. About 10 yards before this ends, turn sharp right over the field.

The area of waste ground indicates where Church Farm used to stand. Where the waste ground starts, turn left on a clear path heading towards houses. On reaching the A650 again, cross it and turn left, but at the end of the houses turn right along a signposted footpath. At the end of the field pass through the facing hedge and bear half right across the next field. Pass through a fence and keep the same direction over the next field. There is a good view of Ardsley Reservoir over to the left. Pass through another fence and keep forward to the wood. Drop by steps and pass along the right hand edge of the wood. At the far end of the wood cross the track diagonally right to find the continuation of the path. Follow it to Westerton Road.

Cross the road and turn right, then turn left along Thirlmere Drive. At the road junction cross the grass and keep forward. Cross another street and continue to a T-junction. Turn left, with the A650 over on your right, and at the end of the street cross halfway over the end of Smithy Lane, then turn right and cross the main road. Turn left, but at the end of the wall turn right down a narrow road and follow it to the end. Turn left along Thorpe Lane, where motorists will find their cars. Bus walkers should walk to the very end of Thorpe Lane, where a tarmac path will return them to the A650 and their bus.

HOWLEY PARK

WALK 3

6½ miles (10½ km); Explorer 288. Almost entirely rural; pleasant woodland and beckside paths and fine views. The entire outward half of the walk follows the Leeds Country Way.

By bus: 218/220 Leeds-Morley-Huddersfield (half-hourly, not evenings or Sundays), 226 Leeds-Morley-Halifax (hourly, not evenings or Sundays). Alight on Howden Clough Road at the top of the hill just after the road crosses the M62 and walk down the road to the "Welcome to Batley" sign at the foot.
By car: On the A643 Morley-Gomersal-Cleckheaton road shortly after crossing the M62 there is a hill down to Howden Clough. 30 yards before a sign says "Welcome to Batley" and opposite the entrance into Howden Clough Industrial Estate there is a large layby on the left. Park here and walk down to the Batley sign.

Immediately after the "Welcome to Batley" sign go through a kissing-gate beside a large gate on the left and take the broad track into the woods. Ignore all paths branching to right or left. After a time the track narrows to a footpath. Cross a stile and continue along the path and soon you have an open view over the valley of Howley Beck to the right. Eventually the path widens to a track again and you cross a stile by a gate. Follow the track to the B6123, turn right for a short distance, then cross and walk along Howley Mill Lane.

About 30 yards before the lane passes through a tunnel under the railway (Leeds-Dewsbury-Huddersfield line) fork left up the access road to a house, but bear right in front of it to cross the railway (care!). The path bears slightly left up the slope. At the far side of the field bear left uphill on a clear cross path. Near the top of the hill the path bears right before the spoil heaps. In a few yards keep left at the fork on the broader path. Ignoring a good track turning left, keep along the foot of the slight rise, and at the next fork keep left to reach the sparse ruins of Howley Hall.

From the ruins descend a little to join a broad cross path and bear left along it. Over to the left is Howley Hall Golf Course, but soon you have a wood 40 yards to your left. A stile to the left of a double metal gate leads onto land reclaimed from mining: follow the fence on your right. Pass a redundant stile and keep on along the fence. When the fence bears right, the path keeps forward. On reaching a tarmac turning circle, walk down the tarmac lane, pass through a stile and turn left along the road, which can be very busy with lorries going to and from a quarry and large waste tip.

In 40 yards find an unsignposted but clear footpath on the right. The deep cutting on your right is the track of a former railway. After a time the tower of Woodkirk Church appears ahead. The path leads to a track: keep on with a cricket ground on your left, then bear right with the

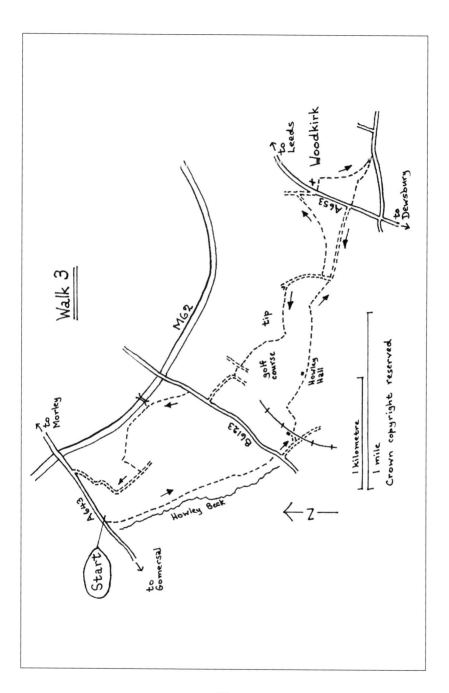

Walk 3

to Morley

to Gomersal

Start

A643

M62

B6123

Howley Beck

golf course

tip

Howley Hall

to Leeds

Woodkirk

A653

to Dewsbury

←—N—→

1 kilometre
1 mile
Crown copyright reserved

track to reach the A653 opposite Woodkirk Church. Cross the main road and enter the church grounds, to follow a paved path past the church, and pass through bollards into a field. Walk straight down and turn right along a cross track at the bottom. Ignore a bridge over the beck, but 30 yards further on fork left on a clear path down to the beckside (easily missed!) and follow this charming beckside path, crossing a stile on the way, until in a field corner you reach a footpath sign.

Ignore the path continuing by the beck on the left and turn right to walk up the left hand edge of the field, with another beck on your left. Pass Scargill Wood and reach the A653 again up a flight of steps. Cross and turn right for a few yards, then turn up Quarry Lane. Once again you are exposed to the

Woodkirk Church

lorry traffic you encountered earlier. Follow the road up past the spot where you joined it before and the end of the footpath you took down to Woodkirk, and keep on along it until it forks near the quarry entrance.

Take the fenced path on the left of the wide gate, and when the tarmac section ends, keep on down the fenced path towards a wood, with a huge waste tip on the right. On reaching the trees the golf course is ahead but you turn right, still following the high fence. This section of the route can be overgrown in summer and the smells can be less than pleasing. Eventually you emerge onto the golf course. Keep forward across it with a broken hedge on your right. Shortly you have trees on both sides and you pick up a track. Follow it to a cross track: keep straight forward to follow a ditch and hedge on your right to the golf course access road. Turn right along this and follow it to the B6123.

Turn right along the footway for about 170 yards, then cross the road to the signposted stile opposite and walk half right across the large field to a stile on the far side. Keep your direction over the next field to reach the boundary fence of the M62. Bear left along this. There is an extensive view left. Ignore a bridge over the motorway and keep along the fence until the clear path enters a wood and bears left away from the motorway. Follow the path through the wood, and when you emerge you have a field on the left and the wood still on the right.

At the end of the field on the left the path turns sharp left as a headland track. On reaching a broad cross track, turn right along it and follow it back to the A643. It is only a few yards to the bus stop, but car drivers will have to cross the road and turn left down the footway to return to their starting point.

MORLEY AND CHURWELL

WALK 4

5¼ miles (8½ km). Explorer 288. A relatively rural ramble on the southern edge of the city, with some fine views to the city centre.

By train: Leeds to Morley (Huddersfield Line). Cross the line by the footbridge and turn left up the access road.
By car: Park at Morley Station (GR 270 282). If the station car park is full, there is room to park on the approach road from the town. From the car park walk uphill past the station on the left.

The first few minutes of the route are not particularly attractive! At the top of the hill turn left along Valley Road, ignore the steep flight of steps at the end and turn left and then left again, to walk downhill, still with the station to your left. Continue past the Orcol fuel depot. Towards the bottom of the road fork right up a grit track with a high fence to your left. Keep right at another fork and follow the stony track up and then down again to a cross path, where you keep forward to cross the railway line (CARE!). Cross the stile on the far side and bear right along the track.

Now the quality improves, and you are in pleasant countryside. Soon your track climbs, to reach a cross-track on a bend. With Broad Oaks Farm over to your right, bear left along the track. There is a view right to the city centre, and the houses ahead are Churwell. The track bends left and then right again and climbs gently to reach the A643 at the south-western end of Churwell. Turn right along the main road. Pass All Saints Church and Shenstone House Surgery on the right and Daffil Road on the left and 20 yards further on turn left up a signposted ginnel. The path passes between gardens and new houses.

Just after you pass a wooden barrier the tarmac path bears left: fork right off it, downhill. Ignore a path forking right at a triangle of grass, and a little further on ignore another path forking right at another triangle of grass: bear left to reach a barrier and a road. Cross straight over and through another barrier and continue along this attractive path. The path soon crosses a side beck by a footbridge. Climb gently through pleasant woodland to reach a tarmac cross-path and bear right down it to cross the beck and climb a flight of steps. Pass through a barrier onto a street: cross it and bear left. At the end of the street keep forward along a tarmac ginnel directly under the power lines. Cross the next street to find the continuation of the ginnel, and when you reach a tarmac lane turn right, then almost immediately left to cross the bridge over the M621.

At the next junction turn right along the tarmac lane and cross the stile by the large gate. Pass to the right of Hill Top Farm and keep forward on the track. Cross a stile and continue on the path, in a few yards meeting a tarmac path coming from a tunnel under the M621 on the right. Turn left along a clear but narrow path. A few yards after the

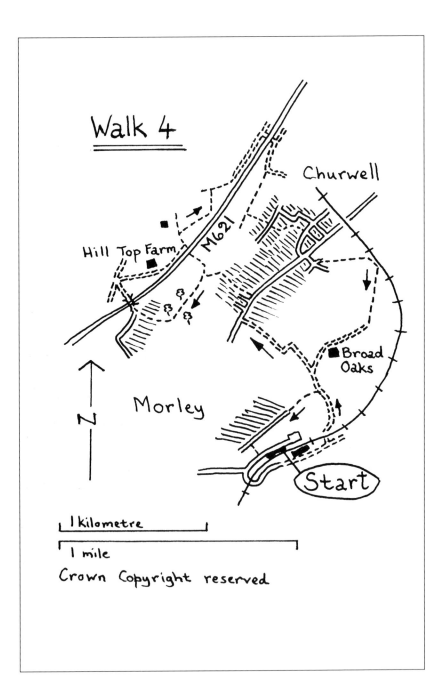

Walk 4

Churwell

Hill Top Farm

M621

Broad Oaks

Morley

N

Start

1 kilometre

1 mile

Crown Copyright reserved

start of trees to the right of the path, go right at a fork and follow a clear path across the middle of the field. Well over the field the path bears left, to pick up a hedge which it keeps on its left. Follow this hedge until you reach a cross path, and here turn right, keeping a fence on your left. The path becomes a tarmac lane with the M621 above you on the right. Cross a stile and turn right to pass under the M621.

Turn right at the T-junction. The track bears left and in a few yards you reach a stile by a gate. Cross this and immediately turn right along a grit track. Where this ends, a clear path forks left towards the end of a hedge. Keep this hedge on your left, and ignoring a path forking left through it follow it until your path also leads through the hedge and up a bank ahead. At the top of this there are several paths: turn sharp left, up towards a fence, then bear left, keeping the fence on your right. When the path reaches a track, bear right along it, with allotments to your left.

Cross over the first street and keep forward along a ginnel. When you reach a cross path, bear left along it. Ignore a paved path forking right, but soon your path bears right, with the garden of Churwell W.M.C. to your right, and reaches a road. Turn right and follow the road up and round to the left to reach the A643 again. Churwell War Memorial is on your right and the Old Golden Fleece is across the road, also to your right. Cross the main road and continue forward along Little Lane.

At the fork keep left, and immediately fork left again down a track. This leads to a stile by a gate. Cross this and keep forward along a clear path, to cross two stiles in facing fences, then walk straight over the next field to the railway embankment. Turn right along the edge of the field, ignore a tunnel under the railway and keep forward for another 50 yards, to where a path forks half-right across the large field, heading slightly to the right of a tall pylon and well to the left of the farm buildings. When you draw level with the pylon you reach a track.

Follow the track towards Broad Oaks Farm. Pass to the right of a large barn. Ignore a left fork to a bungalow, pass to the right of the farmhouse and keep forward along the track. When the track sweeps right, fork left off it downhill on a stony track, now back on your outward route, but where the track bears left at the foot of the hill fork right off it on a clear but narrow path across the field, towards a pylon behind some bushes. The path soon bears slightly left and climbs the slope, leaving a shallow valley to the right. Keep forward parallel to this valley (Don't be tempted down into it), and pass an old stone gateway into a hedged way. When you reach a track keep forward along it, and eventually it becomes a tarmac road. There are fields on the left. Immediately before the houses on the left, turn left down a signposted footpath. It bears right, and Morley Station is down below on your left. At the next road turn left downhill to reach it.

FARNLEY PARK TO GILDERSOME

WALK 5

7¾ miles (12½ km); Explorer 288; some built-up areas, but plenty of fine countryside with remarkable views; a section of the Leeds Country Way. Farnley Hall is a Georgian mansion standing in a park which belongs to Leeds City Council and which is worth a stroll in its own right.

By bus: *No 66, 66a, 67 from Leeds Central Bus Station to Hall Lane (hourly); walk back along Hall Lane and turn right into Farnley Hall grounds, continuing up the access road to the car park.*
By car: Park in the car park in the Farnley Hall grounds just off Hall Lane (GR 247 324).

With your back to Hall Lane and the large expanse of grass in front of you follow the broad path along the left hand side of this, by the trees. When the path forks, bear left through the middle of a wood and emerge from the Hall grounds through a large gateway. Turn left to the road and left along the road. In 50 yards cross a stile on the right, just before a track leading to a sports ground, and walk along the left hand edge of the field.

Farnley Hall

22

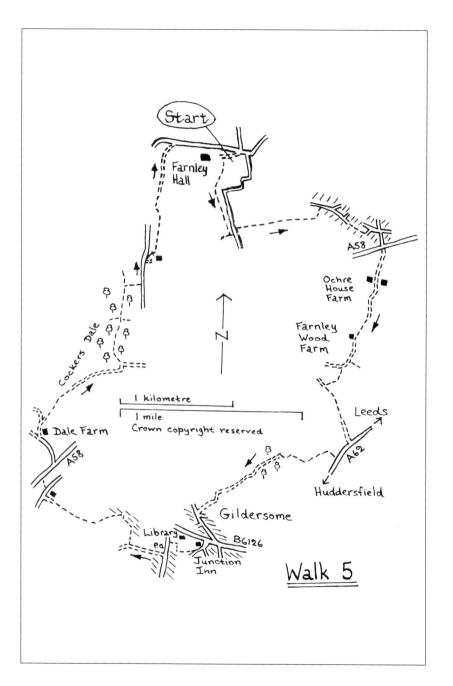

Start

Farnley Hall

Cockers Dale

N

1 kilometre

1 mile

Crown copyright reserved

Dale Farm

A58

A58

Ochre House Farm

Farnley Wood Farm

Leeds

A62

Huddersfield

Gildersome

Library Pd

B6126

Junction Inn

Walk 5

Cross the next stile in the far corner and continue along the left hand edge of the next field. Cross another stile and keep forward with the hedge to your left, at the end of this field crossing another stile, climbing up the low bank ahead, then dropping down the other side and keeping forward along an old hedged way (this section can be overgrown and the path is not clear). In a few yards you meet a good path coming from the playing-fields on the left. Bear right along this, soon picking up a fence on your right with trees and a drop beyond, open ground to your left. The path becomes a broad track. When this begins to descend there is a good view over Leeds Ring Road in the dip ahead to Upper Wortley on the hill beyond. Keep forward down the slope to join a paved track coming from the left.

When you are faced by a metal fence turn left and follow the fence down. At the bottom turn right along the street and where it forks keep right along Cobden Road. This part of Leeds is known as New Blackpool. When the road bends left at Cobden Street keep straight forward with houses on the left and allotments on the right. There are traces of paving. Soon you pick up a tarmac path: follow it forward, ignoring paths sloping up the high embankment on the right, and then follow the footway as it bears left to a T-junction. Turn right (Cow Close Road) and at the next junction again turn right, uphill, to reach the A58.

Cross the main road and turn right, in a few yards turning left up a broad concrete access road which soon bears right. Follow it to Ochre House Farm and walk straight through the yard, out the other side and on uphill. From the top there is an extensive view back towards Leeds city centre. When you draw level with a large shed on the right, ignore the concrete track forking left through a gate, cross the stile ahead and keep on the narrower concrete track which bears half-left across the field. At another stile by a gate the concrete ends. Keep straight forward across the next field towards the left hand end of the buildings of Farnley Wood Farm.

Leave the field through a gate and bear left for a few yards to the next stile. Continue down the tarmac access road. Where this bears right, cross the stile on the left and keep your previous direction across the field to pass under a double row of power lines and cross a stile in the fence ahead. The views are remarkably extensive. Bear right along the right hand edge of the field until at the end you meet a cross-track. Turn left on it downhill. At the foot it crosses Farnley Wood Beck and leads up through trees to a stile and the A62.

Turn right and walk past St.Bernard's Mills, a collection of workshops and warehouses, and 50 yards further on follow a footpath sign which points right into the field. Walk along the right hand edge of the field, but in 100 yards, by a wooden pylon, the path makes a sharp turn left and follows the line of pylons across the field. With two of the pylons still to go, the path bears half-right - it is a very clear path across this very large arable field - to reach the far side of the field close to yet another wooden pylon. Bear right along the edge of the field and in the next corner cross a sleeper bridge, then keep along the left hand edge of the next field.

At the far end of this field the path bears slightly left. Keep forward, ignoring a large metal gate on the left and a gateway opposite, cross the small beck ahead (there may be the remains of a sleeper bridge), pass to the right of a very large old stone gatepost and keep on the clear path along the old hedged track (to judge by the size of the hedges the path is of some antiquity).

Cross a stile, and sections of the path have a brick surface. A yard or two before a stile the path forks: keep right and cross the stile and the cross-track, and keep forward along the track opposite. This continues up the slope, climbing quite steeply - there are

Gildersome War Memorial

long views back - and at the top you are joined by another track from the left. At the next fork keep left along a narrower path (the track leads down right to a farm and there is a trig point in the field on the left), and soon the old hedged lane leads down past a converted chapel to Gildersome. Walk down the hill to a T-junction and turn left to reach the village green.

Just before the War Memorial turn right over the corner of the green, cross the main road and walk along the street opposite, passing in front of the Junction pub. Ignore a footpath sign just past the Co-op pointing left, but 50 yards further, just before you reach a chemist's shop on the right, fork right along a cinder track, and a few yards further on, left into a ginnel. The ginnel turns sharp right, then sharp left again, to reach the next main road. Turn left, but cross the road and just past the post office turn right along a tarmac lane. You have now joined the Leeds Country Way.

The tarmac is succeeded by a dirt track between hedges. At its end go through the stile to the left of the bungalow. At a fork 100 yards further on keep right. Pass through a stile by a gate and follow the path as it heads for the houses. There is a fine open view left to Drighlington. Soon you have the gardens of the houses to your right. Keep along the edge of the gardens until you pass through a squeeze-stile, then turn left through a barrier and keep on down a clear path.

Having come to the end of the houses the path continues with a hedge to the right, soon dropping quite steeply and bearing left to cross a stile and the valley of Andrew Beck, which emerges here from the ground at a spring. Climb the steps on the far side and bear right to the signpost. Now bear half-left across the field, away from the valley, to a prominently marked stile in the fence ahead. Having crossed this, keep forward with the fence to your right, but look out for a stile in it, cross this and turn left, now with the fence to your left, but after passing a hawthorn tree bear half right to pass to the right of a wooden farm building. Now keep forward to a gate in the fence ahead, in a few yards cross a stile by another gate and pass between the houses. Turn right at the road, but in a few yards fork left into a fenced path, which leads to the A58.

Cross and turn right. Immediately after the Valley Inn fork left down Dale Road. At the foot of the hill where the tarmac ends bear right over the beck and pass Dale Farm. After 100 yards fork right again through a stile by a gate, leaving the Leeds Country Way. Where the main track bears right into a field with a collection of farmyard antiques keep straight on, still on a clear track. The wooded Cockers Dale is down to your left. A short distance further on don't be tempted into the field on the right, keep straight forward. Cross a metal stile and keep forward on a clear path across the middle of the next field. Don't be tempted to fork left into the trees. Soon you are again following a hedge on your right, which leads to a stile by a gate and a hedged lane. There is a nice view over Cockers Dale. Keep on the track until you reach a T-junction.

Turn left through the kissing-gate and walk down the track. Ignore another kissing-gate on the left which leads to a path down into the woods, and keep on the clear contouring path with the steep drop to your left. Ignore a path forking right by a bench and a few yards further on ignore another one through a stile and down some steps on the left, and another waymarked path on the right a few yards after that. Keep on along the contouring path, but take the next path forking right uphill (it's easy to miss, but there is an iron fence corner close above you on the right), soon with the fence to your right, to pass through a stile at a junction of fences and follow a fenced path uphill to a stile and the main road.

Cross the road and turn left along the footway. In just over 200 yards ignore a farm access road on the right, but 30 yards further on cross the signposted stile on the right and climb the bank, turning left, first with a hedge, then the Farnley Hall boundary wall on the right. The view left to Pudsey is impressive. Cross a stile and keep forward by the wall. Eventually you pass through another stile and join the tarmac Green Lane, which you follow back to Hall Lane, where you bear right to return to the starting point.

PUDSEY TO FULNECK AND PUDSEY BECK

WALK 6

6 miles (9½ km); Explorer 288; a walk of great variety, good views, fine architecture, woodland and beckside paths. Fulneck shop & restaurant serves snacks and refreshments 9.30-15.00 Tuesday-Saturday.

By bus: No.4, 5, 14, 40 *from the Mayfair Bingo behind Leeds Central Bus Station to Pudsey Bus Station (frequent). Walk through the car park behind the bus station and pass to the left of Pudsey Leisure Centre, keeping forward to the next main road;*

By car: Park in the centre of Pudsey behind the Swimming Baths and Leisure Centre (GR 223 333). On the opposite side of the car park from the children's playground you will see a long high redbrick wall; make your way over to it and turn left alongside it, passing to the right of the Leisure Centre, and turning right at the T-junction down Crawshaw Hill to the main road.

Cross the main road and bear right, but take the first street on the left, Robin Chase, a no through road with modern houses. At the bottom, between numbers 29 and 31, keep forward for a few yards to a lamppost where you turn right along a path with chippings onto the old railway line. Keep forward along this between trees; the cutting is a superb spot for blackberries in season; it can also be muddy after rain.

When you reach the end of this section, bear right for a few yards and cross the main road, keeping the bridge to your right, to find a stile and the continuation of the path along the track of the railway. Pass through another stile and cross straight over the road, again keeping the bridge on your right, to another stile and the continuation of the path. Pass through another stile, cross over the end of the tarmac road, this time with the railway bridge to your left, to another stile and a clear path bearing right alongside the old track. The next stile brings you out onto a tarmac ginnel: turn left for a few yards to the road, then go left over the railway bridge.

In 50 yards you will see a signposted public footpath on the right, a paved path. Follow it past a football pitch, and after the paving ends keep on along the tarmac path, passing to the left of a children's playground. Pass through a metal kissing-gate, cross a street and follow the tarmac path forward to reach the next main road by the side of the Regent pub. Cross straight over and walk up Hillthorpe Road. At the top of the hill, in

Fulneck

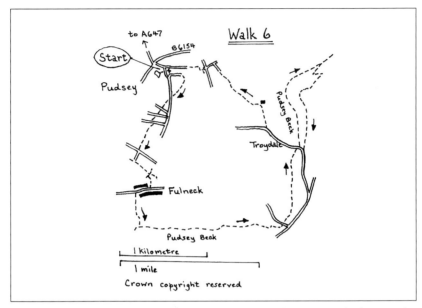

front of the house called Hillthorpe, turn left along a track, but at the gates of Fairmont fork left off the track along a ginnel.

Cross straight over the next track and continue along the ginnel. At the next street turn right for a few yards, then left along a broad track, which soon bears right and soon over the wall on your left you have the first of the many fine views encountered on this ramble: over Pudsey Beck to Tong, then further left over Cockers Dale and Troy Dale. Pass between bollards and descend to the 18th century Moravian settlement of Fulneck, a haven of peace and worth exploring.

Turn right along the split-level road, but where the railing on the left ends turn left down towards a small car park. (A few yards further on is Fulneck shop & restaurant, where refreshments are available.) Pass to the left of this on a road bearing right downhill, but just before you reach the corner of the modern redbrick building ahead, find a set of steps forking left downhill on a paved path, soon with Fulneck Golf Club on both sides. On the way down the path makes a slight bend to the left. Keep on down, and with the golf course immediately ahead walk straight down across it (care!), keeping well to the left of a solitary tree, to Pudsey Beck, turning left alongside the beck and joining for a short time the Leeds Country Way.

At the end of the golf course cross the stile and follow the path through a patch of waste ground. Essentially you are going to follow the beck to the next main road, but fences seem to come and go on this section and the route of the right of way is not always clear. I have described the path as it was in June 2000! Cross another stile into a field

28

Fulneck

and follow a shaky fence on the left. At the end of the fence you can see the next stile ahead, but you have to cross an unpleasantly wet patch to reach it. The first few yards of the next field can also be very wet, but then you follow the fence on your right, but when it curves right, following the beck, keep straight on, to pick it up again a short distance further on. Soon the next stile is visible, at the right hand end of the hedge ahead.

A short section of enclosed path leads to a gap-stile into a yard. Cross the corner half right, pass through a gap in the fence and bear left with the beck on your right. Cross a stile into a field. The right of way continues by the fence on your right, but again this can be very wet. The path is clear to the next stile, after which you continue by the fence on your right. A stile in the fence ahead is followed in a few yards by a stile in a short section of wall. Look slightly left to see the next stile, which leads into a narrow section of fenced path. Leave this over another stile and walk straight across the field to a stile to the right of a gate.

Now you have a fence on your left. Near the end of this field pass through this fence and now keep it on your right. Soon you pass through the fence again and keep it once more on your left. Look out for a section of double fenced way on the left, walk along it, and at the end turn right and bear slightly left to the next stile. The next stile leads into a large field: walk straight across this to a stile, from which the path is clear to the next main road, Roker Lane. Cross it and turn right downhill.

About 20 yards before the T-junction take the signposted path on the left down a flight of steps and follow the path with Pudsey Beck on the right. After a time you reach a stile: cross it, ignore the stile on the left, and continue by the beck. Go through two barriers, ignore a gap in a concrete fence and bear right to pass through a kissing-gate into Troydale Picnic Area. Follow the wall on the left to another kissing-gate then keep on the path to the road at Troydale.

Turn right along the road for about 100 yards, then mount a few steps and pass through a gap-stile on the left into the woods. Keep forward near the bottom edge of the wood, with Pudsey Beck now down on your left. Pass a redundant stile and keep forward through the woods. You lose the beck for a time. Keep the high slope on your right. Emerge from the wood into an open grassy area: keep along the right hand edge of this, then climb gently through the wood on a broad path, which is soon contouring high above the beck. You emerge from the wood into another grassy area: walk across this to the far side, then ignore a broad, gently climbing track turning sharp right, but 30 yards further on take a clear footpath turning sharply back on the right.

Route-finding now becomes a little difficult, there are so many paths. Essentially you are heading for the top of the hill, where you will turn right. So, at a fork of sorts keep left and climb gently over a small open grassy area. On meeting a better path coming up from the right, turn left uphill. On reaching the trees, this path forks: keep right. In a few yards you meet a clear cross path: turn right along it. When you reach another clear cross path, turn left uphill and at the top of the hill turn right with a hedge on your left. The clear path stays close to the top edge of the wood.

Soon the path bends left and there are fine views to Pudsey. Keep always on the path closest to the top edge of the wood, ignoring the first broad path forking right downhill, but when your path begins to drop, keep on the main path, down through the middle of the wood. Keep straight forward and climb once more to the edge of the wood at a fence corner. Cross the stile and keep forward, again close to the top edge of the wood, until you reach a fork. Take the right-hand, main branch, which descends away from the edge and soon becomes a stepped path leading down to the road a short distance from where you first entered the woods.

Turn right along the road. In the dip there is a café. Follow the road until in the bottom of another dip there is a signposted path on the right. (Looking ahead here, you may see ostriches in the fields.) Follow the enclosed path to its end at a track coming from a large house on the right (Acres Hall). Turn left up the track, but just before a fence starts on the right, fork right off it on a clear path which proceeds parallel to the fence (on the left). Pass to the left of a stone gatepost and keep along the left hand edge of the next field. Shortly after you reach houses, the path leaves the field, passing between the houses to a street.

Turn right. At the turning circle at the end keep forward along a tarmac ginnel to a metal barrier. Cross over the track and take the footpath opposite, in 4 yards keeping left at a fork. At a point where you meet several old stone gateposts, keep forward and follow the path over scrubland to a metal stile in a fence. Cross and walk forward along the street. At the end turn left, and at the turning circle keep straight on up a cobbled ginnel. Cross the next street and walk up Greenwood Row. When you are faced by a wall and fence, turn right along the tarmac path, and at the end turn left up some steps and along a ginnel. Go through the old tunnel under the railway and walk up the following street. You reach the main road on a bend, beside St. Andrew's Methodist Church. Turn left past the church, cross the main road, and at the far end of the car park turn right to return to the starting point.

POTTERING THROUGH PUDSEY

WALK 7

5 miles (8¼ km); Explorer 288. Exploring the pleasant Green Belt between Leeds and Bradford; woodland and beckside walking, old tracks, urban ginnels, and a superb panorama of Leeds.

By train: The walk starts at New Pudsey Station.
By car: Park at New Pudsey Station.

From the circular flower bed at the entrance to the station take the track on the left, which leads up to the Ring Road. Cross this with great care, go through the gap by the gate opposite and bear left up the path. After 120 yards look out for a path forking right into a walled lane. Follow this to its end at a street. Cross to the footway opposite and turn left. Turn right down the second street (Sunnyridge Avenue), and at the T-junction at the bottom again cross the road and turn left, but in a few yards fork right down Bradley Lane. At the bottom bear left with the tarmac before the houses of Moorhouse Place, and on reaching a T-junction turn right down the tarmac lane.

At the bottom bear left with the tarmac - Tyersal Beck is over to the right - but a few yards before it leads through large metal gates into Pudsey-Smalewell sewage works fork left off it uphill on an unsurfaced track. Ignore a private road forking right, and the track narrows to a footpath. It soon bends left and climbs through woodland. Pass through a stile by a gate and turn right down a steeply descending track (Tyersal Lane). Cross Tyersal Beck by the clapper bridge and climb up the other side. Pass through what used to be a railway bridge, pass Black Hey Farm and climb to Tyersal Hall at the top of the hill.

When you reach the high boundary wall/fence of Tyersal Hall Farm, your way goes through the stile on the left, but it is worth continuing for a short distance for a glimpse of the fine old Tyersal Hall, built in 1621, on the left. Through the stile, follow the wall/fence, then the field edge, to enter Black Carr Woods (and Bradford District) through another stile. Descend some steps, cross Carr Beck and bear left to reach a broad cross track. Turn left along it and follow it through the woods, ignoring minor paths forking left and right, until you begin to drop more steeply by broad steps. The track leads down to a beck, which you cross by a bridge, then keep forward over a cross track to cross a footbridge over Pudsey Beck (and re-enter Leeds District).

Bear right with the beck to your right, and keeping always as close to the beck as you can (there are several forks) you will reach a stile onto a track with a footbridge a short way off on the right. Turn left up the track to Bankhouse with its remains of old paving. Enjoy fine views over the valley to Tong Hall. A few yards before the Bankhouse Inn turn left along a stony track with the pub car park to your right. Soon you will see and follow a public footpath sign pointing over a stile by a gate on the right (notice the old well here). Follow the track uphill to another

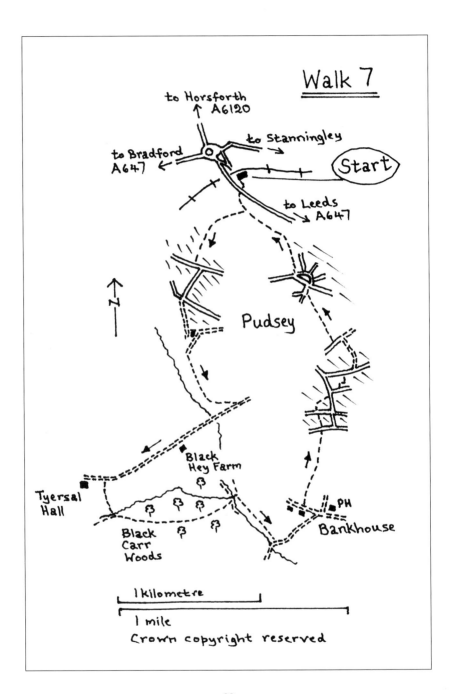

Walk 7

to Horsforth
A6120

to Stanningley

to Bradford
A647

Start

to Leeds
A647

Pudsey

N

Black
Hey Farm

Tyersal
Hall

PH

Black
Carr
Woods

Bankhouse

1 kilometre

1 mile

Crown copyright reserved

signpost, where you bear right, keeping straight uphill on a clear narrow path. Pass through a gap-stile and continue up the narrow ginnel. From the highest point there is a magnificent view over Leeds.

Descend the ginnel, cross over the first street and keep on along the ginnel opposite. Cross the next street and continue ahead along Smalewell Close: the footpath leads forward and then bears right to reach a main road. Turn left here, but go right into School Street. When the tarmac ends keep forward past Pudsey United Reformed church, and immediately before the tarmac begins again turn left along a narrow footpath, which soon turns right along the back of a terrace of houses. Watch out for a chance to turn left and walk along the side of the Golden Lion car park to the pub itself, where you bear right then left to reach the main road.

Cross it and turn right, but in a few yards turn left along the unsurfaced Grove Road. Follow this track to its end, then keep forward along the tarmac street. At the junction at the far end turn left, but in 80 yards turn right down a paved ginnel, which leads through Queen's Park. At the end of the children's playground walk along past a car park to a T-junction, cross the main road and turn left. At the end of the grass cross a street and a yard or two further on fork right along a track (Owlcotes Lane). At the end of the track keep forward along the footpath, and when the houses end go through the stile and keep following the wall on the left. There is a fine view right over Airedale. Pass through a stile beside a rusty gate and immediately keep right at the fork. The path leads down to the Ring Road. Cross and return to your starting point.

CALVERLEY CIRCULAR

WALK 8

6½ miles (10½ km); Explorer 288. Easy walking on old tracks and footpaths through pleasant pastoral and wooded countryside, partly on the Leeds Country Way.

By bus: No. 670 Bradford bus from Leeds Central Bus Station to Victoria Street, Calverley (half-hourly; no service in evenings or on Sundays). Or No. 90 from Leeds City Bus Station to Victoria Park, Calverley (hourly). In this case walk up through the Park to the exit at the top (Victoria Street).
By car: In the centre of Calverley is Victoria Park with the war memorial, playing fields, bowling greens and a children's playground; at one corner is the large Methodist church. Park in Victoria Street, which runs along the opposite side of the park from the main road.

Walk along Victoria Street with the park on your left, cross over Chapel Street and pass Parkside School; cross over Thornhill Street into Rushton Street and ignore the next street forking left; cross straight over the next road and continue along Rushton Street; when you reach a T-junction turn right, then turn left at the next crossroads. In a few yards ignore a footpath sign pointing left, but at the end of the road take the signposted bridleway (Shell Lane) on the right. Now you have left the built up area.

Soon a fine view opens up left over the Aire valley towards Leeds. After some time the path bears right and climbs to a cross track: go straight over into the signposted bridleway opposite. This path soon bears left and reaches another cross track. Turn right along it. This is Priesthorpe Lane, which you follow all the way to the Leeds Ring Road, passing at one stage Calverley Golf Course and later Priesthorpe School. At the ring road bear right to the large roundabout and there again go right towards Bradford; this section is noisy and smelly and boring, but it doesn't last long.

At the next roundabout cross straight over Woodhall Lane, the Pudsey to Calverley road, and continue in the direction of Bradford. About 40 yards after passing the barracks, 5 yards after passing underneath a road sign, turn right between bollards (here you join the Leeds Country Way) and walk along the right hand side of the grassy area, keeping straight forward as far as you can go to find a stile, which leads left along an enclosed footpath with playing fields now also to the right.

Keep with the fence when it bears right, and when you see a very clear path a yard or two to your left, join it and bear right along it through pleasant woodland. Immediately after passing through a gap in a facing fence fork left to a gap-stile, then follow the clear path straight across the field to a gap in the far wall and keep forward to the left of an old field boundary. Cross a stile and bear slightly right to enter an enclosed path with the golf course to your left. Pass through another stile onto the golf course. Your way now lies straight forward, over a number of fairways, where you should keep a look out for flying

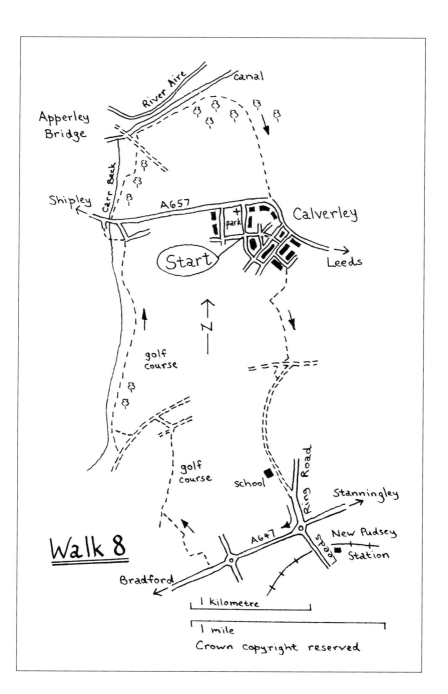

River Aire

canal

Apperley
Bridge

Carr Beck

Shipley

A657

park

Calverley

Leeds

Start

N

golf
course

golf
course

school

Ring Road

Stanningley

Walk 8

A647

New Pudsey

Speen

Station

Bradford

1 Kilometre

1 mile

Crown copyright reserved

missiles, eventually to pass through another stile by a gate into a walled lane.

In 30 yards ignore a stile by a gate on the left, but a few yards further on keep left at a fork down a fenced track with a large deep quarry to the left and follow it down to a gap in a wall and a broad walled track. Turn left down this. Look out for an old stile on the right (opposite an entrance into the quarry) leading onto a clear descending path under two sets of power lines. Go down the broad path to a cross track.

Turn right along this and ignoring all paths and tracks forking left and right follow the main track down the valley (Carr Beck is down to your left) until shortly after you are joined by a wall on the left you pass a large mill and go through a stile by a gate onto a road. Keep forward for 25 yards, passing the entrance to the mill, then take the signposted ginnel on the left. Cross the beck by a footbridge and bear right along the track. Pass a charming corner with some stone built cottages (Carr Bottom) and keep on up the lane, cobbled for a short stretch.

Carr Bottom

Cross straight over the main road at Greengates and go through the gap in the wall to the right of Carr Bottom Road. The path drops steeply by steps and soon reaches the beck side. Follow this delightful woodland path by the beck until it bears right uphill along the edge of the wood with a wall to the left. When you reach a broad track go left along it, keeping left when it forks to cross a stile by a gate and bear left down the tarmac lane. But only for a few yards, because before you reach the bridge over the Leeds and Liverpool Canal you must fork right down a track (here leaving the Leeds Country Way) which bears left to a small marina. Just before you reach the canal turn right (between two buildings) through a stile by a gate, then in a few yards cross another stile and keep forward with a high fence and the canal to your left.

Follow the clear track forward: it soon starts to drop towards the canal, but before it reaches it you must cross a stile on the right and walk along with a fence to your left and the wood to your right. Soon the path is a few yards inside the wood, parallel to the canal. Shortly after passing under a pylon the path bears right away from the canal, but still close to the edge of the wood. Shortly after the path begins to climb gently, look out for a path forking left to a stile in the wall on the left. Cross this and keep right along the top side of the field. There is a fine view across the canal to Cragg Wood and Rawdon. Soon another stile takes you back into the wood. Rejoin the path you were on earlier, go left, but immediately keep right at a fork on an ascending path away from the edge of the wood. Join a track and bear right uphill. For a short distance you have a high wall to the right.

Now it is easy to get lost. Pass an old gatepost. A track comes in from the right: bear left for a few yards, then fork left off this track, but then immediately right again (in spite of the yellow arrow!) on a narrow ascending path with the track you have just left down below you on the right. Keep along the edge, with the drop to your right, then bear slightly left with the path to reach the left hand edge of the wood; keep uphill on a clear path with the wall and fields to the left. About 25 yards after reaching the edge of the wood find a stile in the wall on the left, cross it and bear right up the outside edge of the wood. Now your problems of route-finding are over.

The clear path leads round to a cottage, with a stile on the left immediately in front of it. Keep down the field with the wood to your right. The tower of Calverley Parish Church is visible ahead. Go through a gated stile beside a large gate and keep forward with a playing field to the left, then Calverley School, to reach the main road. Bear right along it, and when you are opposite the Methodist church cross the road and go up Chapel Street to the left of the church. Soon there is access to the children's playground and the park. There is an exit from the top side of the park onto Victoria Street.

CALVERLEY, FARSLEY, RODLEY
AND THE CANAL

WALK 9

7½ miles (12 km); Explorer 288. Field paths, old urban ginnels and a stretch of canal towpath.

By bus: No. 670 Bradford bus from Leeds City Bus Station to Victoria Street, Calverley (half-hourly; no service in evenings or on Sundays). Or No. 90 from Leeds City Bus Station to Victoria Park, Calverley (hourly). In this case walk up through the Park to the exit at the top (Victoria Street).
By car: In the centre of Calverley is Victoria Park with the war memorial, playing fields, bowling greens and a children's playground; at one corner is the large Methodist church. Park in Victoria Street, which runs along the opposite side of the park from the main road.

Walk along Victoria Street with the Park on your right, but cross the road where convenient. At the crossroads cross straight over Hollin Park Road, in a few yards turning left along a track. Cross over the next cross street and take the enclosed path to the left of Calverley Medical Centre. At the end bear left through a works car park, then continue along the mill access road. Go straight over the next cross road to take the stile to the left of the bus shelter. Walk half right up the field (there is a faint path), pass through a hedge and follow the same line to the next stile, which is now visible.

Walk straight up the next field to the next stile, then continue with the wall/hedge on the right (there may be Highland cattle here). After the next stile go half left to the next one, reached down a few steps, then bear slightly left over the next field, passing to the left of the power line pole and through the middle of a patch of scrub with thistles. The next stile gives access to a track. Cross this slightly left to a stile and follow the clear path straight over a large field to the stile opposite. Turn right along the track. About 15 yards after the entrance to Priesthorpe Farm on the right cross the stile on the left and walk forward over the field.

Cross the stile and follow the wall on the left down through two fields, then turn right and drop to Leeds Ring Road. Cross this with great care to the path opposite, climb to a stile and follow the left hand edge of the field. Pass between two stone gateposts and bear right along the top edge of the next field into an enclosed path. You are now going to traverse Farsley. At the end of the path go half right across the tarmac lane and into another ginnel, with a cricket ground over the wall on the right. At the end turn left along the street and follow it as it bends right, then turn left at the T-junction. At the next T-junction turn right up Town Street.

Pass the Old Schoolhouse and School and the Victorian Parish Church, then the Library, cross over South Drive, then cross the main road and go left along Frances Street, to pass Westroyd Infant School. At the T-junction turn right, but just after Claremont Nursing Home turn left

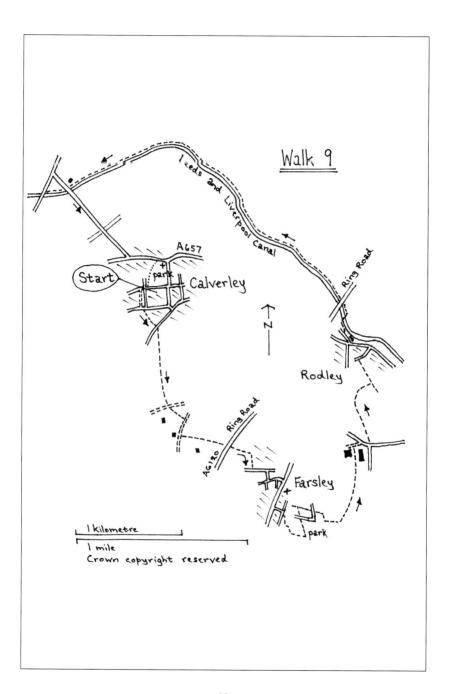

Walk 9

Leeds and Liverpool Canal

A657

Start

park

Calverley

N →

Ring Road

Rodley

Ring Road

A6120

Farsley

park

1 kilometre

1 mile

Crown copyright reserved

into Westroyd Park, where many benches, roses and flower beds invite one to pause for a rest. Pass to the right of the sad old mansion, bear right to the bowling green, but turn left before it to follow a tarmac path to the far end of the Park. Turn sharp left there with the path, and having passed some high garden fences on the right, leave the Park along a tarmac ginnel.

Cross over the next street and continue along the ginnel, pass through a barrier, cross another street and turn right along the tarmac path by the recreation ground. At the far end cross over Parkside Road and keep on along the tarmac ginnel opposite. This turns right by Farsley Recreation Centre, and at the next street turn left along a concrete track with a cricket ground on the left. When the track leads through a large metal gate, fork left off it, then in 10 yards keep left at a further fork on a path which leads you down the valley of Farsley Bottoms. At one point you cross the bottom of a tarmac path.

On reaching a fork, ignore the tarmac path climbing left and keep forward on the unsurfaced path, unpleasantly spoiled by rubbish, which passes to the left of a mill. When you join a better path, keep forward along it. Pass through a barrier onto a cobbled lane at Broom Mills, with The Skep Mill Shop on your left. Turn right up the lane, passing Beck Bottom Cottages, and on reaching the main road, cross it and turn right uphill. Opposite Half Mile Lane on the right turn left along a clear footpath. A good view of Farsley opens up. The path bends right between two old gateposts, then immediately goes left again.

On reaching the next open grassy area, bear left along its edge, but where this edge bends right, fork left along a clear path. Soon the view is over the Aire valley to Horsforth and Rawdon. Follow the path down, and on reaching a clear cross path, turn left along it past a bench. Turn right down the next street into Rodley. At the T-junction at the bottom turn left along Town Street (A657). Fork right along Canal Road, and immediately after the Rodley Barge turn right up to the canal and walk along past the moorings to cross the swing bridge. Turn left along the towpath.

Follow the towpath for nearly 2¼ miles (3½ km) to the modern bridge 214A. Just before it climb the steps on the right to the A658 and turn right along the footway. Turn right along Parkin Lane and at the next fork keep left uphill. Cross the canal bridge and walk straight up the track (Calverley cutting), ignoring all tracks branching off to left or right. Near the top you pass through a deep cutting and under a bridge. Turn left at the A657 into Calverley. The pedestrian crossing at the post office will take you back to Victoria Park.

(Another walk which you might like to try is the Calverley Millennium Way, a 7-mile circuit around the village. A booklet describing the route, with much additional historical information, is on sale at the Post Office and in local shops.)

HORSFORTH CIRCULAR

WALK 10

8.85 miles (14¼ km); Explorer 288; a most attractive and varied walk, using woodland paths in the NW Leeds built-up area, riverside paths, and field paths with distant views; the only drawback is that several busy roads have to be crossed.

By train: Leeds to Horsforth (Harrogate Line). Having arrived by train from Leeds, make your way to the main road.
By car: The car park at Horsforth Station is for rail users only. Park considerately in nearby streets.

Cross straight over the main road (Station Road) to walk down Troy Road. Pass the Low Lane Car Centre and 50 yards further on turn left down the tarmac drive to the Brookfoot Estate, keeping by the wall/fence to your right until you join a footpath to the right of a large factory building. Cross the beck and keep straight forward through the wood, turning right along an old cobbled cross path with a wall to the left. A short distance along look out for a path forking left off the main path through an old stile into a walled ginnel with the railway immediately to the left. Where it ends go left under the railway, then immediately turn right off the tarmac path onto a clear path which in a few yards joins a broad path forward through the woods. Bear left away from the railway, with houses over on your left.

This path in turn joins another tarmac footpath along which you bear right, but in 50 yards fork right off it on a clear path down into the woods. Ignore minor paths forking left and right, and your path will bear right to pass under the railway again. Bear left on the broad woodland path, which passes to the right of the noisy Tweed House boarding kennels. A few yards before you reach the bridge over the beck turn sharp left uphill, still to the right of the kennels, then bear right on an ascending path back into the woods. The path soon for a short distance follows the edge of the wood with fields on the right. About 20 yards before the track leads under the railway again fork right off it on a clear path which soon has a wall to the left and fields to the right. Follow this to the Leeds Ring Road.

Cross the Ring Road with great care and turn left, passing under the railway yet again, then immediately turn right on the signposted path on grass, with the fence, wood and railway to the right, and enter the woods on a narrow ascending path up Butcher Hill. Soon you are higher than the railway, with Abbey Grange School to your left. At the main road turn right, crossing the railway for the last time. Ignore a road forking left, but 50 yards further on take a ginnel on the left, which leads to Cragside Close, where you bear right. The street soon bears left, and just after this bend a path on the right leads into Hawksworth Woods. In a few yards keep left at a fork, and when you reach a clear cross path bear left along it with a valley to your right. Ignore paths forking right or

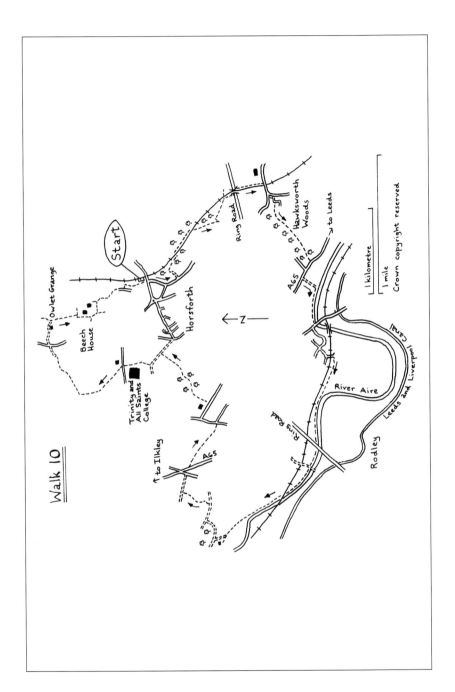

Walk 10

Start

Owlet Grange

Beech House

Trinity and All Saints College

Horsforth

← N —

to Ilkley

A65

Ring Road

River Aire

Rodley

Ring Road

Hawksworth Woods

A65

to Leeds

Leeds and Liverpool Canal

1 kilometre
1 mile
Crown copyright reserved

left and eventually you will be led down to the A65 opposite Gate 2 into Kirkstall Forge.

Again you have a busy road to cross with great care, then turn right along it. A sign soon tells you that you are entering Horsforth once more. Immediately after the first house on the left turn left down a stony track (bridleway sign). Cross the old Kirkstall Forge Goit just before the track bears right, and now you are close to the river Aire. After a time you can hear and glimpse the weir on the left at which the mill race starts. Walk forward along the track. At the T-junction the cobbled Newlay Bridge, erected in 1819 and one of the oldest iron bridges in the county, is to your left, but your route turns right up the road, here joining the Airedale Way.

After 50 yards turn left along a narrow concrete road. The lane becomes tarmac and soon curves right uphill. Ignore streets forking left off it. Climb to a T-junction and turn left along Newlaithes Road. Where the new houses on the left end, turn left down an unsurfaced track, cross the railway and at the end of the bridge turn right along a fenced path. The view half left is across to Rodley. Pass through a kissing-gate into the field on the left and keep your direction as before.

Near the highest point a bench provides a pleasant view up the Aire valley. Drop to another kissing-gate and the river bank. At forks keep left by the river. Pass under the Ring Road and again keep left at a fork. Calverley Lane Picnic Site is up to your right. The path soon leads up a few steps to a stile onto an old cobbled lane. To the left is the stone Calverley Bridge over the river, built in 1776 after the great flood of that year; crossing it would lead in a few minutes to the Railway Inn at Rodley. Cross over the lane to the stile opposite.

Soon you pass under a pylon and follow the direction of the power lines. Cross a stile and pass under two railway bridges, then continue along the riverside path, which can be very overgrown in summer. Cross a footbridge and follow the path until you join a wall on the left, after which another path comes in from the right. This section can be very wet. Go left here. When you reach a modern house, pass to the right of it up the access road (here joining the Leeds Country Way). When you meet a cross track go right, and at the next T-junction again go right, once more on tarmac. At a junction of several roads and tracks bear sharp left up a path between hedges, soon passing through a barrier. This old walled path is a fine place for blackberries in season. Shortly after passing through another barrier turn right along a stony track, and at the first tarmac road turn left up to the A65 again.

Turn right, cross the road again with great care and in about 100 yards go through a signposted gap in the wall on the left and down the steps into the field. The path leads across the corner of the field to a stile into the woods. Cross Gill Beck by the footbridge and climb steeply up some steps and into a hedged footpath. Where this ends go through the gap-stile and keep forward with the remains of a hedge to your left. There is a splendid view over Airedale. Keep forward and at the far end of the field bear right still with the hedge to your left. Follow the hedge round to a stile, cross it and follow the hedge on your left to another stile and then to another stile by a gate. Keep forward, soon between hedges, to another stile into a ginnel.

At the road turn left, then left again at the T-junction, then take the first road on the right (West End Lane). Immediately past West End School go through the stile on the left into woodland. When you reach a fork with a couple of sleepers on the ground and the main path going straight ahead uphill, fork right onto a narrower path, also uphill. You are joined by a path from the left; keep forward, to pass a wooden pylon in the middle of the path, and at the next fork (a tree between the paths has a painted waymark) keep left uphill, and at the next junction of paths keep straight forward uphill, parallel to the edge of the wood and a wall closeby on the left. Keep on the main path over Hunger Hills and leave the wood over a stile, to walk along the edge of the field with the hedge to your left. The view over Leeds is excellent.

Lee Lane Farm

Go through the stile by the gate onto Lee Lane. Turning right here and then bearing left at the bottom would be a short cut back to Horsforth Station, but your route turns left along with the wall to your left. A few yards before the tarmac road at Lee Lane Farm turn sharp right (footpath sign) into an enclosed path, down towards the running track in the grounds of Trinity and All Saints College. Turn left along a paved path, which is almost immediately joined by another paved path from the right, but where the paved path goes through a gate turn right along a hedged path, with the college buildings to the left, and follow it to Brownberrie Lane.

Cross the road into the drive to Brownberrie House, but in a yard or two go through the stile in the wall on the left and follow the clear path through the wood. Go through a kissing-gate in the middle of the wood, and on reaching the far side of the wood ignore a stile on the left and keep along close to the edge of the wood. Just before you reach the far corner of the last field on the left, keep left at a fork, and having passed this field corner, the path keeps straight ahead through the wood. Leave the wood over a stile and walk forward along the right hand edge of the next field. On reaching a cross wall, turn right and keep this wall on your left. Cross a stile and cut the corner of the next field by walking along the row of airport approach lights, to return to the wall on your left. Keep with the wall until your only exit is over a stile in it. Bear right down the tarmac lane.

At the foot cross straight over Scotland Lane and bear left down the farm access road opposite. Pass to the left of Owlet Grange and immediately after it fork right (footpath sign). At the end of the track cross the step-stile in the wall on the left and walk forward a few yards to another stile. Here you part company with the Leeds Country Way, which turns left, for you go right along the edge of the field with a wall to your right. Pass through a gap in a cross wall and at the end of the next field cross the stile and walk forward with a hedge to the right. At the far end of this field, with a wood ahead, cross a stile onto a track: ignore the first track to the right, walk forward a couple of yards and take the second track to the right, which soon bears left with a wall to the left.

Pass the entrance to Beech House on the left and keep forward along the track (footpath sign). At the end of the wood on the left leave the track by crossing a stile on the left and walk down the left hand edge of the field. When you reach a gate on the left with a stile beside it, bear threequarters right across the field to a stile in the wall on the far side. Cross the sleeper bridge beyond and keep forward with the fence to your left to another stile in the wall ahead. Over this bear half left down the next field to a stile a yard or two up from the far corner. Walk straight across the next field to the next stile, then forward along the street for about 50 yards to find a ginnel on the left between the houses. At the bottom of this bear right along the track, which leads to Horsforth Station.

HORSFORTH TO CRAGG WOOD AND RAWDON

WALK 11

5½ miles (9 km); Explorer 288. An easy walk of great variety and interest, with urban ginnels, field paths and mature woodland.

By bus: 33 Leeds-Yeadon-Otley (hourly, not Sundays), 732/733/734/736 Leeds-Otley/Ilkley (every 10 minutes, evenings every 15 minutes, half-hourly on Sundays) to the junction of Rawdon Road (A65) and Hall Lane Horsforth.

By car: Park in the large Hall Park car park off Hall Lane, Horsforth. Walk to the far end of the car park and start the walk at [*].

Go down the unsurfaced track on the opposite side of the main road from Hall Lane. When you reach a surfaced road, keep forward down it, but take the first road on the right (Low Hall Road) (Low Hall is the fine old house you glimpse on the right just before you turn right. Low Hall Farm, a short way along, also has some fine buildings). Where the road bends fairly sharply right and widens out, take the right fork, between industrial buildings, and where these end, keep forward up the track. With houses ahead turn left, cross a footbridge and turn left down another track, but immediately after an old chapel on the right, now a private house, cross a stile on the right and walk round the right hand edge of the field.

Low Hall Farm

Go through a small gate, keep down the edge of the next field, cross a stile at Woodbottom Farm and keep forward up the farm access road. Follow the track up to a junction and turn left along a tarmac drive. Keep on it for quite some distance, passing large houses and the mature woodland of Cragg Wood, until it begins to descend very gently and you fork right off it up a broad unsurfaced track, which becomes dark from the overarching trees. At a junction take the second track on the right (the first is the entrance into Daisy Hill), follow it up to the next junction, and ignoring the entrance into The Coach House, turn right along a tarmac drive with Rawdon Golf Course to the left.

In 200 yards ignore a road forking left along the side of the golf course and keep forward along the tree-lined avenue. Pass the entrance to Buckstone Hall, where the tarmac ends, but follow the avenue to its

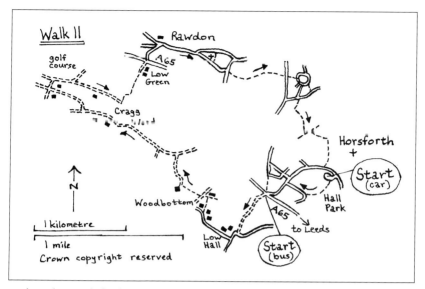

end and turn left along a path which soon passes round a padlocked gate. There follows a delightful stretch of grit footpath. Pass round another gate at the far end and walk up the lane through Low Green, noticing the Friends School built in 1898. Cross the A65 (there is an island just to the right) and walk up Well Lane opposite.

At the top of the hill, with the Emmott Arms opposite, turn right along Town Street, Rawdon. Follow it all the way to the Parish Church and take the first entrance into the churchyard. Here are the old village stocks. Walk up towards the church and turn right in front of it. At the end of the paved path go through the gate on the left and walk up the left hand edge of the recreation ground, past the Jubilee Hall, and out onto Layton Avenue. Turn right and follow it to the T-junction at the end.

Cross the road and turn right along the footway. Immediately before the next junction cross a stile on the left and walk down the fenced ginnel. On reaching a track, cross it diagonally right, pass through

Rawdon Stocks

another stile into a field and walk down its left hand edge. Part way down the field the path forks: keep left, drop a few yards to another stile, then walk straight down the field, cross Gill Beck and walk straight up the other side to a stile in the top corner. Keep along the right hand edge of the next field, cross another stile and continue by the hedge on the right. Keep forward over a broken down wall in the next corner, then walk straight across the middle of the next field.

Rawdon Church

Cross the next road diagonally right to the ginnel opposite, which leads to a street. Turn right, cross the end of two streets, one very narrow, the next rather wider, then between the houses 55 and 53 turn right along another short ginnel. At the next street again turn right, but 50 yards after it bends right, cross and take a signposted footpath on the left. It passes through a narrow strip of woodland before dropping to reach a clear cross path. Turn left on a gently climbing path near the left hand edge of the wood.

In 100 yards keep right at a fork, 20 yards further on keep right at another fork and 5 yards further on keep right at a junction, on a path which descends through the wood towards houses. Keep straight on at the next cross path - the houses are a short distance off on the right - then keep along parallel to the houses, near the bottom edge of the wood, until you reach a clear cross path (Horsforth Parish Church is straight ahead). Turn right on a path which drops gently, cross straight over a narrow tarmac path, and on reaching an open grassy area, walk straight down with the wall on your right, but when this turns right, keep straight on over the grass to a gap in the wall at the foot.

Cross the road and turn left along the footway, to find an entrance into Hall Park on the right. Walk down the broad drive to pass flower beds and an old fountain. The path narrows and passes between trees: bear left with it to reach the car park. Here motorists will find their cars. Turn left past the car park (the bowling green is half left) then [*] walk straight forward over the grass to a gap in the wall you can see on the far side. Leave the park, cross the road and turn right up the footway. At the T-junction at the top cross the road and turn right, but turn left along the first street (West End Rise) and again take the first street on the left (West End Grove).

It soon bends right, but where it bends right again, fork left off it down a ginnel. This leads down to the A65 at its junction with Hall Lane. Motorists will cross the A65 to the track opposite and go back to the start of the walk description.

48

RAWDON BILLING AND CRAGG WOOD

WALK 12

5 miles (8 km); Explorer 288; airy views, woodland and riverside; some paths, including the one by the river, can be overgrown in summer.

By bus: _No. 732/733/734/735/736 Otley/Ilkley bus from Leeds Central Bus Station (every 10 minutes, evenings every 15 minutes, Sundays every half hour) to Rawdon cross-roads._
By car: _Park in the car park by the library and council offices at the top end of Micklefield Park, on the A65 Leeds to Ilkley road a few yards on the Guiseley side of the junction with the A658 Bradford to Harrogate road (GR 208 397)._

Return to the traffic lights and walk along the Harrogate Road on the right hand side of the road. About 70 yards from the lights turn into a signposted ginnel on the right in the middle of a terrace of shops and climb the steps up Pease Hill. On the way up you cross over one street and at the top you cross another, continuing forward along the pavement. Cross yet another street and keep forward along Peasehill Park to re-enter the ginnel, which you follow to the next main road, crossing a tarmac drive on the way. Cross the main road and turn right along the footway. At the roundabout bear left past the Emmott Arms, then take the first street on the left (Billing View).

Follow the tarmac up, ignoring Billing Court on the right, and bear right at the top, forking left along a track just before a terrace of houses (still Billing View). At the end of the houses keep forward along the track with a small reservoir to the right. The track soon narrows to a footpath between hedges (a fine place for blackberries in season), and when it opens out again by some upright posts, fork left uphill towards the wood. When you reach a cross path turn left up it and follow it round to a stile. On your right is the reclaimed quarry of Rawdon Billing, which you may like to explore, and extensive views open up to the left. Cross the stile and walk forward along the edge of the bank on a clear path, before bearing slightly right in the direction of the trig point.

But when you reach a fence corner by a hawthorn bush on the left, well before the trig point, turn sharp right and walk down the field with a hedge to your left. When the hedge ends keep on by the wall, bearing right with it at the bottom of the field to pass through a gateway in the far corner. Bear left downhill parallel to the hedge/wall on your left. Cross the stile by the gate in the bottom corner and walk forward to reach a kissing-gate onto the playing fields at Rawdon School. Keep forward behind the goalposts to reach a tarmac path which passes to the left of the wall enclosing the school playground, then bear left round the bottom edge of the car park to reach Town Street, Rawdon.

Cross and go down Carr Lane opposite. About halfway down, by a lamppost, go right along a signposted ginnel, which leads you down to the A65. Cross this busy road with care and take the farm access track to

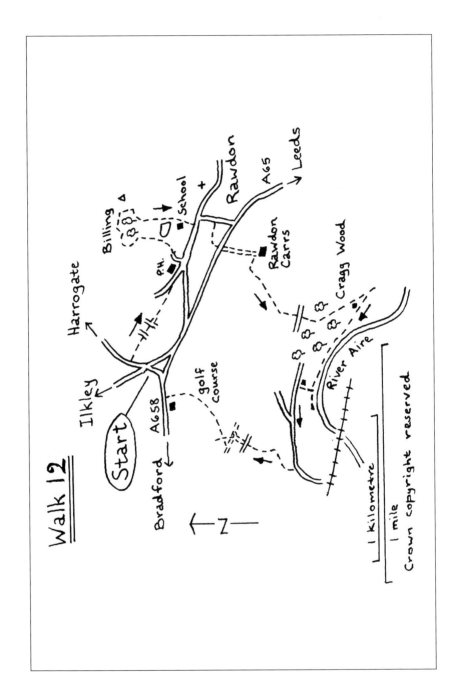

Walk 12

Rawdon Carrs opposite. Go through the large gate into the farmyard then immediately cross a gap-stile on the right. Walk straight across the field to another gap-stile in the wall opposite, then half-left down the next field to a stile to the left of a gate. Now bear slightly right down to the next stile some 10 yards to the right of the trees in the bottom of the field, then keep the same line down to another stile into a narrow strip of woodland. Bear slightly right through this to another stile, then walk straight down the next large field, passing to the left of a low embankment, to a stile by a gate.

Cross over the tarmac road into a walled ginnel opposite. At the end of this keep forward for a few yards with the wall to your right to a stile, cross it and walk straight over the field to a small gate on the far side, then go down the steps and bear left over rough ground to join a track. Turn right down this, soon with an overgrown wall to your left. This area, sloping down to the river Aire, is known as Cragg Wood. Pass round a gate and cross a track, to descend the tarmac lane opposite. Pass to the left of a modern house then fork right, down towards a metal gate, but before you reach it turn right down a fenced path to a kissing-gate, then keep forward between a fence on the left and the wood on the right. Parts of this path can be overgrown in summer. Soon you are close to the Aire.

Follow the riverside path until, shortly after crossing a section of boardwalk, you turn right up an enclosed footpath by wooden steps. Pass to the left of houses and turn left along the tarmac lane. Join a wider road and keep forward along it. Where the road bends left, with houses ahead, turn right up a tarmac drive (bridleway sign on the lamppost), and at the next cottage fork right into a walled lane. Soon it bears left and you ascend between high walls.

When you reach a junction of several drives, keep straight forward uphill in the broad walled lane. Look out for a narrow walled ginnel forking left off it and follow this up to a tarmac drive. Cross over this and continue up the ginnel. When you reach the next broad track turn right along it. Ignore the entrance into Grange Thorpe on the left and follow the track straight across the middle of Rawdon Golf Course (caution!), bearing left to reach a tarmac road beside the golf club car park. Bear right up to the main road, and turn right again there. Soon there is a gate on the left into the park, which you can explore before returning to the starting point.

YEADON TARN, RAWDON BILLING
AND SPRING WOOD

WALK 13

6¼ miles (10 km); Explorer 288. This is a walk I particularly enjoy, it has so much variety and interest. Woodland tracks, field paths, urban ginnels and several splendid viewpoints.

<u>By bus:</u> *No. 732/733/734/735/736 Otley/Ilkley bus from Leeds Central Bus Station to Rawdon cross-roads (every 10 minutes, evenings 15 minutes, Sundays 30 minutes) and turn left into Micklefield Park.*
<u>By car:</u> *Park in the car park by the library and council offices at the top end of Micklefield Park, on the A65 Leeds to Ilkley road a few yards on the Guiseley side of the junction with the A658 Bradford to Harrogate road (GR 208 397).*

Walk down into Micklefield Park between the council offices and the library and keep straight forward along the tarmac path. When you reach the tennis courts, turn right, and at the next junction turn left, and leave the park through a gap in the wall ahead. Keep forward along the grass by the track, and when the tarmac street starts, along the footway. At the T-junction cross diagonally right and walk down London Street. This part of Rawdon is known as Little London. Cross the main road and turn left, but turn right down the left hand edge of the car park of the Princess pub to a stile. There is a fine view left to Thackley, Baildon, Rombald's Moor and much more.

Walk down the left hand edge of two fields, go through the small gate on the left and bear right, to follow the wall on your right to the next stile. Continue by the wall on the right, but when you reach a short section of walled lane, do not enter it, but turn left and follow the hedge on the right down to a stile in a short section of wall ahead. Go through and follow the fence on your left, passing a redundant stile, to a small gate in the next field corner. Cross the next field diagonally right to join a track in the far corner, which you follow down to Ghyll Fold Farm. Go through the stile on the left of the large gate ahead, then walk diagonally across the yard, noticing the fine old farmhouse, and bear right down the access road.

Turn right up the next road, but take the next minor road on the left and in 100 yards turn left along a track. After a time you pass to the right of Calverley Close Cottage and cross the Leeds-Ilkley railway by a bridge. In a few yards keep left at the fork along a narrow partly cobbled path which descends with a wall on the left and enters Spring Wood as a walled lane. At the next junction keep right. The path curves right and is joined by a track coming from Esholt Sewage Works on the left. Soon Guiseley Beck is down on your left. Ignore a track forking left to a stile by a gate and ignore a high railway footbridge on the right.

Cross the beck by a bridge and pass through a tunnel on the Bradford-Ilkley line.

In 80 yards look out for a path forking right off the track through a stile by a gate. A clear path leads across rough grassland and climbs to a fence. Keep the fence on your right until you reach the houses, then turn right to cross the railway by a footbridge. Turn left and follow the tarmac road through the industrial estate to the A65. Cross it and turn right. Cross the end of Nunroyd Avenue and continue until the start of a wood on the left. Cross the wall on the left and follow a clear path through the trees, soon crossing a wooden footbridge. Just after it ignore a path forking left and keep along uphill parallel to the wall on your right to reach a grassy area and a grit running track. Bear left along the left hand edge of this, pass the metal barrier and bear slightly right over the grass towards the stone house.

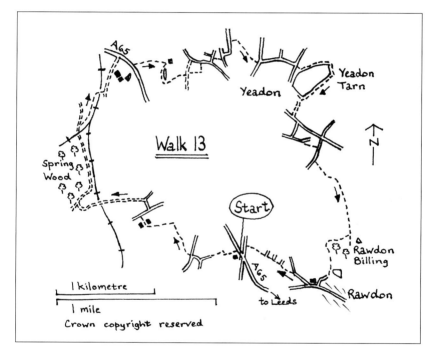

Follow the tarmac drive to the right of the house and where the tarmac ends turn right and follow the path along with the lake on your left. At the far end turn left over the footbridge and walk up the grass to pass between a wood and a line of trees. Keep forward to pass behind the goalposts to a gateway in the fence ahead. Keep forward along the track, pass through another gateway and turn left at the T-junction. In a short distance turn right into another park and follow the tarmac path forward through it. Keep straight on at a cross path, pass to the left of the children's playground, then bear left and follow the path to an exit in the corner on the right. A paved path leads to the next road (Shaw Lane). Cross and turn right.

Take the next street on the left, Coppice Wood Avenue, but in a short distance, opposite the next street on the left, go up a paved ginnel on the right. Cross the street at the top and turn left, but in a few yards turn right up Banksfield Crescent. Follow it as it curves left, then between houses 38 and 40 turn right up a hedged path and go through the stile at the top onto Yeadon Banks. Keep forward up the steep slope and turn right along the fence at the top. Pause here to enjoy panoramic views. When the wall ends and the fence turns left keep straight forward over the grass, aiming to the left of a short terrace of brick houses, to a stile onto a road. Cross it and bear slightly left up Hawthorn Drive opposite.

At the end cross straight over at the T-junction, go through the gap in the wall and walk forward to join the path round Yeadon Tarn. Walk clockwise round the Tarn to the far right hand corner (looked at from here). When the fenced embankment starts, fork left past the boatyard and walk along the left hand edge of the car park, then out to the road. Cross and turn left, but take the first street on the right, Windmill Lane. Turn left along Grange Avenue, but where it bends left, just after passing some lockup garages, fork right along a ginnel, which leads to the A658. Cross and turn right. Turn left along Moorfield Drive, keeping straight forward to the end, where a short ginnel leads to a stile into a field.

Walk very slightly left across the field to a stile in the fence opposite, cross the track and the next stile and follow the left hand edge of the field until a hedge begins on the left, where you bear half right over the field to a stile in the far corner. Walk straight down the middle of the next field to the next stile, now on a clear path, then straight up the next field to a stile near the top left hand corner. Follow the fence on your left up to the corner, then turn right on a clear path which soon follows the top of the slope to a stile (very fine views). The path now leads round the wooded summit of Rawdon Billing. After a time fork right on a clear path down over grass towards a stout wooden post. A narrow hedged path leads down to a track, which passes to the right of a small reservoir and a short terrace of houses.

Bear right along the tarmac road, then go left with it to reach Town Street in Rawdon. Turn right past the Emmott Arms and bear right at the roundabout. Between houses 54 and 44 on the left, almost opposite a works entrance on the right, turn left along a ginnel. It crosses a tarmac drive and reaches a street: keep forward, crossing two streets to find the continuation of the ginnel. It leads downhill, crossing another street on the way, to the A658. Turn left to the crossroads, cross the A65 and turn right for a few yards to return to the starting point.

YEADON TO OTLEY CHEVIN

WALK 14

8¼ miles (13¼ km), Explorer 297; an easy stroll to the ridge between Airedale and Wharfedale, with fine views on both sides. The return is by field and woodland paths, ending up with a walk round the perimeter of Leeds & Bradford International Airport, with a good view of the main runway.

By bus: _No. 655, 755 (half-hourly, hourly evenings and Sundays), 731 (half-hourly, infrequently on Sundays as 729), 735, 736 (every 10 minutes, half-hourly evenings and Sundays) from Leeds Central Bus Station to Yeadon Town Hall. Note that the return bus to Leeds does not leave from the High Street, which is one-way, but from Harper Lane, which is the road on the top side of Morrison's. From the Town Hall walk up the High Street to the large roundabout, cross it and take Cemetery Road on the left. Pass the New Inn, and 40 yards further on turn right along a grit path with a high fence on the left. It bends left, and when it forks, keep right to the car-park of Tarn Field Park._
By car: _Park in Tarn Field Park car-park in Yeadon. Coming from the A658 traffic lights, you pass on the right the White Swan with Dam Lane beside it and Windmill Lane opposite. The entrance to the car-park is 50 yards further on opposite Walsh Vehicles Repair Limited._

From the end of the car-park pass to the right of the boatyard down to Yeadon Tarn and turn left across the embankment. Follow the bank of the Tarn round until you have a large grassy area on your left. Midway between the third and fourth bench along this, turn left over the grass to a gap in the wall ahead. Cross the road and keep forward along Hawthorn Drive. Follow it to its end, cross the road to the stile opposite and bear slightly right up the field onto Yeadon Banks. Walk along with the wall on your right and extensive views to the left. After contouring for a time, the path forks left down to a gate in the corner of the field where the garden fence ends.

Walk straight across the field to the next gate, an interesting combination of gate and stile: from it keep straight forward to the next gate, then on for a short distance with a wall to the left, but where that bears left keep forward down the field on a clear path to cross a wooden footbridge and a stile into a fenced path. At the end of this pass through a gap-stile and continue with a wall to your right. Cross a stile and continue by the wall on your right. Bear right with the wall and cross another stile by a gate to enter a walled lane, which leads to West Carlton Farm. Here walk straight forward up the tarmac access road to the next motor road, cross it diagonally right and continue along the stony walled lane (Mall Lane). Pass to the left of a bungalow and follow the lane up to the next motor road (York Gate). This is the highest point of the walk.

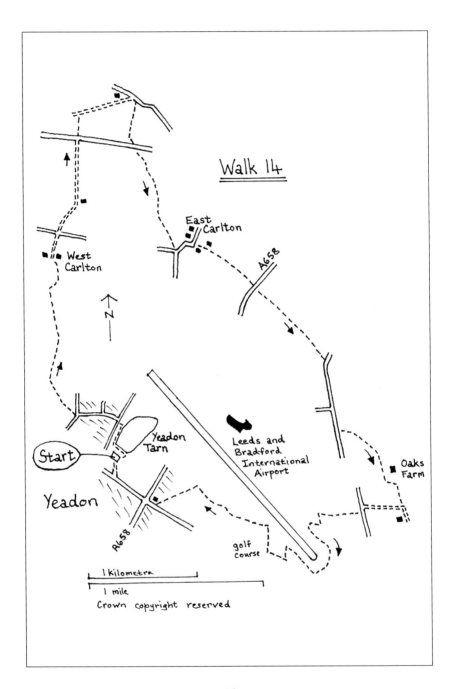

Walk 14

East Carlton

West Carlton

A658

N →

Start

Yeadon Tarn

Leeds and Bradford International Airport

Oaks Farm

Yeadon

A658

golf course

1 kilometre

1 mile

Crown copyright reserved

Again cross straight over into the track opposite. When the track bends right, you can enjoy a fine view over Lower Wharfedale, with Almscliff Crag prominent in the middle distance. At the Otley Old Road turn right uphill for 50 yards to a stile and footpath sign to Carlton. Cross and follow the wall on your left uphill. At the stile in the top corner pause to enjoy the view back, then continue with the wall on your left. About 50 yards before the far end of this field cross a step-stile on the left and cut the corner of the next field to another step-stile a few yards to the right of a gate.

Cross York Gate again and take the track opposite into York Gate Plantation, in a few yards keeping left at a fork. Leave the wood by a stile and follow the left hand edge of the field. Cross another stile and continue by the fence/hedge on your left, which soon curves left to another stile. Cross and walk half-right over the next large field to the next stile. Turn left along the road into East Carlton. Where the road makes a sharp left hand bend, fork right off it down a No Through Road. At the end of the road follow the track through the yard of Carlton Home Farm, but where the track bends left to a barn, fork right off it, with a fence on your right, on a narrow path leading to a stile into a field.

Follow the path across the field to the next stile a short distance away, then continue forward through the next large field, heading for a short piece of fencing in a hedge corner. Pass through the gate to the left of the fence and follow the hedge on your right, then a fence, to the A658 Bradford-Harrogate road. Turn right along this busy road for a few yards, then cross to the signposted footpath opposite. Cross the stile and follow the wall on your left. At the far end of the field cross the stile by the gate and walk along the right hand edge of the next field for 25 yards to a concealed stile and footbridge on the right, then turn left with a fence and wood on your left.

At the far end of the field cross the stile into the wood and follow the clear path through it. Leave the wood by another stile and turn right up the road. Cross a narrow bridge and pass an access road to the airport on the right, then 180 yards further on cross a signposted stile on the left and walk along the left hand edge of the field. Cross a stile on the left and follow the right hand edge of the next field. At the far end turn left with the wall to find a stile on the right. Follow the wall on your right. At the far end of the field pass to the left of three large trees, through a gate and along a track. Oaks Farm is below, with Cookridge beyond. Join the farm access road and bear right along it for 50 yards, and immediately after another track comes up from the left, fork left off the tarmac road on a narrow path which crosses a sleeper bridge and a stile and enters a wood.

Follow the clear path through the wood, which you leave through a gateway. The right of way now turns left and follows the edge of the field round, but walkers are now tending to walk straight over the field to a stile in the wall on the left. Cross and follow the wall on your right.

The valley to the left is that of Moseley Beck. Cross a stile by a gate. Dean Grange Farm is ahead, but you turn right up the farm access road. Turn left along the next road (Scotland Lane) for a few yards, then take the signposted footpath on the right. Walk up the left hand edge of the field until you reach a step-stile in a walled-up gateway. Cross and follow the path through the trees.

The path soon turns left with the airport perimeter fence on the right. Follow this fenced path round the outside of the airport. As you reach the top side there is a fine view of the main runway, and the pleasantly landscaped Horsforth Golf Course is to your left. When the enclosed path ends, keep on along the perimeter fence. Soon a bare area on the left leads to the summit of Plane Tree Hill. Keeping always as close to the fence as you can, you will reach a stile into a field. Walk down the right hand edge and as you near the bottom bear left, to continue along the field edge, passing to the right of a small pond (the ground can be wet here) to a stile. Turn right along the footway to the traffic lights, cross straight over and follow Yeadon High Street back to your starting point.

HAWKSWORTH

WALK 15

7 miles (11¼ km) for those who come by bus, 4¾ miles (7½ km) for motorists; Explorer 297. An easy ramble on clear paths, a mixture of pasture and woodland, with fine views.

By bus: No. 731/732/733 Leeds to Otley/Ilkley from Leeds Central Bus Station (every 10 minutes, evenings 15 minutes, Sundays half-hourly), or No. 33 Leeds to Otley from Vicar Lane (hourly, not Sundays) to the White Cross (near Harry Ramsden's) in Guiseley. Walk along to the White Cross pub. At the roundabout cross over the Bradford Road and Thorpe Lane and go through the kissing-gate by the footpath sign. Follow the path into the narrow strip of woodland, in a few yards turning left at a T-junction. Follow the path until it climbs to a small gate in a wall and a farm access road. Turn right along this, ignore the entrance to Thorpe Farm on the right and go through the gate ahead, and a few yards further on fork left along a track to a stile by a cattle-grid. High Royds Hospital is over to your right. Follow the track to the next farm, cross the cattle-grid just before you reach it and then the stile by the gate to the left of the buildings. Ignore a track forking right and keep forward to the stile by the next gate. Cross it and turn sharp left up the hillside.

By car: Drive to the west end of Hawksworth and continue along Old Lane, straight over at the crossroads and along Goose Lane to its junction with the Bingley Road; turn right here and a short way along on the right is a very large layby: park here, and start the walk description at [*].

The path climbs steeply up the slope, bearing slightly right away from the fence on the left, to a stile in the fence at the top. Cross and walk straight over the large field. There is a fine view back to Menston, Guiseley and the Chevin. As you come over the crest you will see the next stile in the wall ahead, with trees beyond. This leads into an enclosed path which brings you to Hawksworth. Cross diagonally right over the village street and walk down a short track between houses leading down to a white gate.

Cross the stile beside the gate and keep forward through the yard to another stile ahead. Over this follow the path down the field (fine view to Baildon Moor and Baildon), reaching the right hand edge where the fence becomes a wall. Continue down the wall side, crossing three stiles, and now you have a golf course to your left. Keep on down, and just before you reach the trees turn right, cross a beck by a small slab bridge and then another stile. Turn left downhill, now with the wall to your left, to another stile into the woods, and follow the clear path down to the valley bottom, being joined near the foot by a path from the left.

Don't cross the beck by the stepping stones, but turn right over the stile. Follow this lovely woodland path to another stile, then keep forward for a few more yards to cross the beck by more stepping stones. In a few yards the path forks: ignore the stile ahead (signposted White

House) and fork right (signposted Sconce Lane). The path keeps parallel to the beck on the right for some distance before climbing away from it to a stile in the wall on the left. It is in fact a double stile, forward then right, then you bear left up the field edge with a wall to your left to another stile in the top corner.

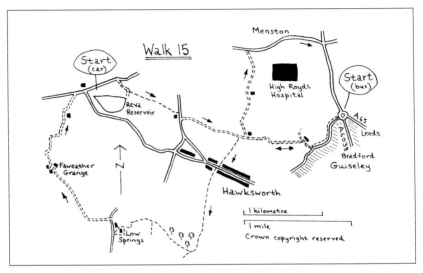

Bear left along the edge of the field, soon bearing right with the wall. When the wall ends keep along the fence. At the end of the fence look out for a diversion through a kissing-gate on the left, leading into an enclosed path, at the end of which there is another kissing-gate, after which you turn right to join the tarmac drive and follow it to the motor road. But at present you cross a gap-stile in the wall ahead into the garden of a house. Walk forward to pass to the right of the house and through a gate in the fence ahead. Continue through the next garden to the facing wall, where you turn left through the white gate and along a ginnel to a tarmac drive.

Bear right up to the motor road and turn right along it. Where the road bends right fork left off it up Sconce Lane, and follow this until it kinks right and then left to pass through Faweather Grange. Having gone through the gate fork right downhill, and shortly fork right again onto another descending track It bears right to a gate, and you cross the beck by

Clapper Bridge

a clapper bridge. Continue up the track, taking care not to bear right off it into the field (there is a signpost). Near the top there are short sections of old paving in this walled track. Eventually you pass to the left of a farm and follow the track to the Bingley Road. Turn right along it, ignoring the next road on the right which leads back to Hawksworth. Car drivers should find their cars in the layby a little further on.

[*] From the layby continue along the wide grass verge in the Menston direction, with Reva Reservoir to your right, and follow the road until you reach a footpath signpost pointing right over a stile by a gate and along a broad fenced track (a notice on the gate says Wharfedale Scout Sailing Centre). Follow the track, but where it bears right down to the reservoir, cross the stile straight ahead and keep forward on the grassy path with a fence to the right. About 30 yards before the fence joins a wall bear left on a clear path parallel to the wall and follow it to a stile in a facing fence/wall. Cross this and bear right with the fence to your right, bearing slightly left when the fence becomes a wall, and follow this wall to another stile in a facing fence. Cross this into the grounds of stables and bear left along the fence on your left to a stile and a road.

Turn right along the road for about 50 yards to a signposted path on the left. Cross the stile, which is immediately followed by a gate, and walk along the track, with a view left to Otley Chevin. The track passes through a gate with a stile to the left of it. For a short distance you are in the remains of an old walled lane. Follow the track as far as the next gate, about 100 yards before farm buildings. Those who came by car will not cross the stile, but will turn right up the slope and jump to the start of the walk description, those who came by bus will cross the stile and walk towards the farm.

High Royds Hall

(For those returning by bus, a pleasant alternative end to the walk would be to walk down to Menston and catch the bus there. So turn left immediately before the farm down to a pair of gates. Pass through and follow the track. Cross the stile by the next gate and continue on the track. The fine old house ahead is High Royds Hall. When you reach the outbuildings of the Hall, pass through the kissing-gate and keep forward down the access road. This leads to the Bingley Road in Menston. Turn right there, and at the next junction keep forward, passing a recreation ground on your left, to return to the A65 at traffic lights. The bus stop for Leeds is a few yards to your right, on the other side of the road.)

GUISELEY TO THE WEST CHEVIN

WALK 16

6½ miles (10½ km); Explorer 297. Field paths, old tracks and superb views. One long, steep climb.

By train: There are trains to Guiseley from Leeds, Bradford and Ilkley on the Wharfedale Line. Those arriving from Leeds or Bradford should cross the line by the footbridge and leave the platform along a fenced ginnel.
By car: The car park at Guiseley Station is for rail users only. You might find a space on the approach road (Station Road), in which case you would need to walk to the station, cross the line by the footbridge and leave the platform along a fenced ginnel. Otherwise take the A65 from Leeds to Guiseley, pass Morrisons's on the left and turn right at the traffic lights by the Station pub; cross the railway bridge and turn left into Netherfield Road; just after leaving the 30 m.p.h. limit there is a large cemetery on the left, and at the far end of this a layby on the right, just before a public bridleway sign on each side of the road. Park here and take the bridleway downhill, starting the walk description at [*] below.

Leave the station platform by the fenced path, and at the end cross the road and turn right. Immediately after the medical centre turn left along a signposted footpath. Cross a street and continue along the ginnel opposite, soon joining a track which you follow to the next road. Cross and turn right, then at the T-junction turn left, [+] passing Guiseley Infant School. Turn left up the next street (West Villa Road). Follow the school boundary wall/fence to where it ends at the cul-de-sac of Willow Gardens and keep on up the road, shortly forking left along a signposted bridleway, which passes to the right of the entrance into Claremont.

At the top cross the street and turn left (Kelcliffe Lane), in a few yards forking right along a track (No Through Road). After a time you pass the entrance into Kelcliffe Mount and continue along a walled lane. Immediately after the wall on the right ends go through a stile on the right and bear half left up the field to the top corner. Cross the stile and follow the fence on the right to the next stile. Cross the next field to a gate in the fence opposite, then walk straight over the next field to a stile by a gate on the right of a building. Pass to the right of Bracken End Farm and follow the access road to a T-junction. Turn left downhill. At the next road, motorists will find their cars on the left. Cross straight over and continue down the lane opposite.

[*] Walk down the bridleway as far as the next farm access road on the right, which you follow to Intake Farm. On reaching the buildings, go through a gate on the right and bear left along the edge of the field to a stile. Bear slightly left over the next field to the next stile, then keep on in the same direction over the next field to the next one, walk straight across the next field to a kissing-gate, then follow an old wall on the right, pass through a gateway ahead and bear slightly left to another kissing-gate and a road.

Cross the road and walk along the track opposite, which passes several attractive houses. At the end pass to the left of Holly Croft Farm, go through a stile by a gate and continue down a walled lane. At the end cross the stile and follow the right hand edge of the field towards Oaks Farm. In the next corner ignore the gate and turn left with the wall to find a stile on the right. Cross it and turn left to follow the left hand edge of the field to a stile in the bottom corner. Follow the path forward, crossing a wooden footbridge, then follow the fence on the right to pass an attractive bend in a beck. When the fence ends, keep forward to follow a hedge on the right to the A6038 in Menston. Turn right along the footway.

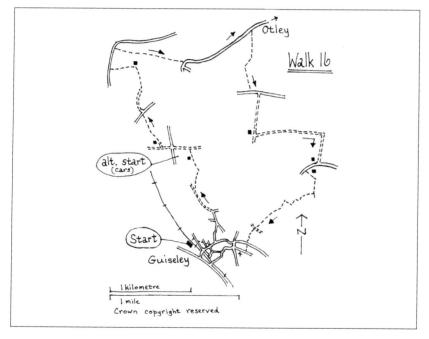

Immediately after an old mill on the right (Imperial Works) turn right up a tarmac drive, but in a few yards fork left off it to a stile and follow the path up with a wall and wood on the left. After two more stiles you are walking just inside the wood. Glorious views open up over Wharfedale, from Burley and Beamsley Beacon to Otley and Almscliff Crag. Follow the path to a stile by a gate and walk straight across the field to the next stile, then very slightly right over the next field to a stile onto West Chevin Road. Turn left along the footway.

Follow the road for about a kilometre, until you have a large field on the left with a gate into it. On the other side of the road there is a large metal gate. Go through the gap beside it and take the path climbing steeply into the wood. A short distance up look out for a fork, where you must turn sharp left. Soon the path emerges from the trees and bends right again, steeply uphill with a fence on the left. There now follows a long pull up, so take your time! After a time the clear path bears right away from the fence and soon enters the wood. Steps help you up the steepest bit, and soon you are not far from the right hand edge of the wood.

Follow the path to the top edge of the wood, cross the stile and follow the clear path over the field to a gap-stile on the far side. Turn left up the road (York Gate) for 80 yards, then turn right down a walled track. Shortly after passing a house on the right, turn left along another track and follow it for almost a kilometre. Just after passing a small cluster of buildings on the left ignore a gateway ahead and turn right, to follow the track down past Upcroft Farm to the next motor road. Turn right along this. Pass a large house called The Grove on the left and 70 yards after it turn left into a signposted stony track.

After passing through a gateway, the track forks: ignore a gate on the right and keep forward with the wall/fence to your left. Shortly before you reach a facing gate cross the stile on the right and walk forward along an old hedged way. This leads to a gap in a facing wall. Ignore the stile on the left here and turn right along the wall, keeping it to your right. When the wall ends keep forward to pass between two old stone gateposts and pass a redundant stile to reach a footpath sign by a facing hedge. Turn left, and keeping a ditch on your right walk down the edge of the field until you come to a wooden bridge over the ditch and a stile in the wall. Cross this and turn left to follow an enclosed path round two fields.

Cross the stile into the third field and keep forward near the left hand edge with a beck to your left. Pass through a gap-stile onto a lane, go left along it for a few yards, but where it bears left fork right off it through a stile and bear right down the field with the wall on your right. Cross a gap-stile in the field corner and continue with the wall on your right to another stile near a gate, from which you follow the wall on your right down to another stile and the main road. You are now back in Guiseley. Cross the road and take the signposted ginnel opposite, turning right along the road at the far end.

Pass to the right of Guiseley Parish Church, cross the main road and go down Well Lane opposite past the Woolpacks Inn. Just before the road bends left you will find on the right Guiseley Wells, the heart of the old township. A short distance further on fork right along Wells Road. Turn right at the end and cross straight over the next street. Rail walkers will keep forward along Ashtofts Mount, motorists will turn right and jump to [+] above. Now you are back on your outward route. In a few yards fork left along a track, and when this bends right keep forward along a ginnel. Cross a street and continue along the ginnel opposite. Cross the next road and turn right to return to the station.

OTLEY TO POOL BANK AND THE CHEVIN FOREST PARK

WALK 17

7 miles (11¼ km); Explorer 297. Otley Chevin is worth exploring in detail - there are lots of paths - and this suggested route is intended merely to serve as an introduction. Clear tracks and paths over pasture and through woodland, with superb views over Lower Wharfedale.

By bus: No. 780 (Otley, hourly, no evenings or Sundays), X84/784 (Ilkley/Skipton, half-hourly, hourly evenings and Sundays) from Leeds Central Bus Station to Otley Bus Station.
By car: there are several car parks in the centre of Otley.

The walk starts at the Jubilee Clock in Otley Market Place. Walk through the Market Place, pass to the left of the Black Bull and along Market Street. At the traffic lights cross straight over and pass to the left of the Argos store (Boroughgate). A few yards after passing the fine Methodist Church, at a small square with a car park, turn right, cross the next street and turn right again (Walkergate) and when you reach a metal barrier on the roadside, turn left along a ginnel. At the next street turn left again along South View Terrace and keep forward until you reach West View: turn right down it.

Pass to the left of a children's playground and at the far end of it turn left along a path between high fences. On reaching a fork, keep left along by the fence on the left, go through a stile and keep forward to pass to the left of some cottages. Immediately beyond them go through a stile on the right of a gate into an enclosed path. At the end of this keep forward over the grass to join a cross track, turn right along it for 10 yards, then cross a stile on the left and bear right, following the path parallel to the fence on the right. Cross the stile at the far end of this field and continue with a fence on your left. Cross another stile, and now the fence is on your right. Near the far end of this field bear left to a stile and turn right along the tarmac lane.

In 100 yards ignore a track forking left. Immediately before you reach Brick House Farm fork right along a footpath. Ignore a wooden kissing-gate on the right and keep forward along the hedged path. Shortly before you reach the embankment of the old Leeds to Otley railway (with a tunnel under it) fork left, keeping a hedge to your left and the railway to your right. At another fork again avoid climbing onto the embankment and keep forward to a stile. Over this turn right through another tunnel (shared by a beck), over another stile, then bear sharp left along the hedge/fence on your left.

There is a view across Wharfedale to Farnley Hall. Cross a stile and footbridge in the corner of the field and keep forward along the left hand edge of the field, at the far end turning right with the fence up to a stile in the next corner. Now bear left, with the fence to your left, which in the next field becomes a wall, which should be followed to a step-stile in a facing wall. Across this bear slightly left towards the left hand end of a row of trees, where there is another stile. Cross straight over the tarmac drive to another stile and follow the fence on your right until you reach a stile in it. Cross this and walk up with a fence on your right to cross another stile into the yard of Caley Hall Farm.

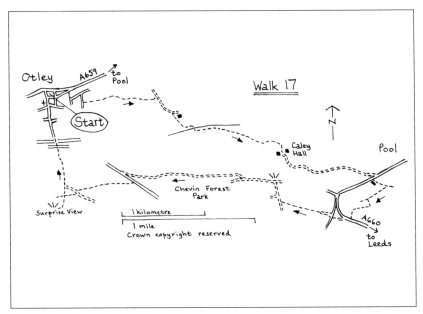

Walk straight forward to join a track which leads through a gateway ahead. Soon you enter a walled lane and pass under power lines. Follow the track and the wall on the left until you have to cross a facing stile, then continue with the fence/wall on your left to the next motor road (Old Pool Bank) (the village below to your left is Pool in Wharfedale). Turn right up the road, but after 150 yards turn left along Sandy Lobby, a row of mock half-timbered houses. When the concrete drive ends keep forward on a clear path along the edge of the wood. Soon the path starts to climb and you reach a junction, with a stile a few yards to the left. Be careful here! Take the path forking sharp right up into the wood. When you reach the back of a terrace of houses bear left along them, then turn right at the end of the row and keep forward to pass to the left of the garages.

About ten yards after the garages fork left on a faint path which climbs towards a fence at the top of the wood and leads to a stile out of the wood beside an old gateway. Cross and walk forward to the wall on the far side of the field, there turning right and keeping this wall on your

66

left to the top corner of this long field. Cross the stile, turn left and follow the track to the A660. Cross with care and turn right. Immediately after the garage fork left up a lane. At the end keep forward along a paved path to a minor road (Old Pool Bank again), turn right for a short distance then left along Quarry Farm Road.

At the end of the road go through the stile by the gate into an enclosed footpath. Pass through a barrier into the Chevin Forest Park and immediately cross a stile on the right, off the boardwalk. On reaching a fence corner a broader track comes down from the left: keep forward along this. Soon a short detour can be made right to Caley Crags. The magnificent view extends from Otley via Farnley Hall with the Washburn valley beyond and the lakes in the old gravel pits at Knotford Nook to Pool, Almscliff Crag and the Weeton railway viaduct.

Now continue along the broad path. Go through a kissing-gate beside a large gate and keep forward along the broad path. At the next major junction fork right downhill. At the foot of the slope ignore a path forking sharp right. Now follow your track all the way to the Otley Old Road, ignoring minor paths to left and right, and passing first through a rocky landscape, popular as a practice ground for climbers, then through woodland. On reaching the road, turn left uphill for a short distance, then right into the East Chevin Quarry car park.

Walk through the car park to a barrier by a large gate, which leads to a broad ascending track. The path is soon contouring, with more fine views over Otley and Lower Wharfedale. You enter woodland and soon reach a broad cross path: turn left uphill. When you reach another broad cross path, turn right. Follow this path until shortly after it levels off you reach a long flight of steps on the right. That is your way back to Otley, but before going down them you might like to take the path on the left, which climbs to the Surprise View, another fine belvedere (with the Royalty pub not far off!).

Now go down the long flight of steps, crossing a narrow path and two broad tracks on the way (the tracks lead to the White House Information Centre). A stile leads into a cobbled path which you follow down to another stile and a junction of tracks at a road end. (On the left is the White House gate into the Forest Park.) Cross into the narrow enclosed path opposite and follow it down to the next road. Cross this to the continuation of the footpath, which leads to a footbridge over the Otley bypass. Go down the steps on the far side and keep straight forward to return to the centre of Otley.

BRAMHOPE TO COOKRIDGE

WALK 18

5½ miles (8¾ km); Explorer 297; easy tracks and field paths with remarkably distant views.

By bus: No. 780 (Otley, hourly, no evenings or Sundays), X84 (Ilkley/Skipton, half-hourly, hourly evenings), 784 (Ilkley, hourly, Sun) from Leeds Central Bus Station. Alight near Bramhope Church and walk along the road towards the church, but just before you reach it go through the kissing-gate on the left by the notice board and follow the tarmac path past the east end of the church. Where the tarmac ends keep forward over the grass, pass through the trees and keep forward, mount the steps and keep on over more grass to a tarmac drive. Follow this forward, bearing left and right with it, to reach Eastgate, there turning left.

By car: From the crossroads by the Fox and Hounds in the centre of Bramhope village take the road signposted to Bradford (Old Lane) and after 60 yards turn right into the free car park (with toilets) (GR 247 433). To start the walk return to Old Lane and turn left along it to the crossroads, there going straight over and along Eastgate.

In Eastgate look out for the attractive 17th century Weaver's Cottage on the right. Immediately after the parade of shops on the right with the post office take the signposted tarmac path on the right. The mound to the left with the children's playground on top is a spoil heap from the construction of the Bramhope railway tunnel in 1846-9, the line of which we shall be following for the next mile. Cross straight over the first street you reach to continue on a clear path, now on top of the mound of spoil. Soon you descend a flight of steps on the left.

The clear path leads forward. Pass to the right of the first of the four tunnel air shafts you will encounter and keep forward with a wall to your right. Pass between two old gateposts and continue to a barrier by some houses. Cross the drive to a stile in the fence, then bear half right across the corner of the field to another stile and the road, there going left. About 20 yards past Moorland Road on the right cross the signposted stile on the right and bear half left, passing well to the left of the second air shaft, cross a stile in the fence and again bear half left to pass between two gorse-covered mounds of spoil. On emerging from these bear slightly left towards the next air shaft, crossing a stile on the way to it. Pass to the right of the air shaft, and the next stile is at the left hand end of the wood ahead. Keep straight forward, soon again between spoil heaps, to the Otley Old Road.

Cross diagonally right to the stile opposite into a fenced footpath. When you are faced by a wooden fence ahead turn right along it. In this fence you will come to a short section of wall with a stile in it: cross this and bear half right up the field, in the direction of the fourth and last air shaft, to a stile in the top corner. Turn left to cross a stile by a gate, and when the fenced track ends keep forward up the right hand edge of the field. At the far end cross a stile into a fenced path and pass to the left of Crag House Farm. At the end of the enclosed path cross a stile by a gate and turn left along the farm access road.

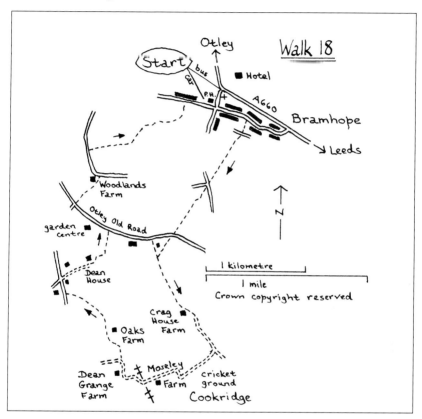

When you reach the grounds of Cookridge Cricket Club turn right along the tarmac lane, keeping the cricket ground on your left. When the tarmac bears right into Kings Lea, keep straight ahead along the dirt track. The track curves right, then left again. Pass to the right of Moseley Farm and downhill, to cross Moseley Beck and the Leeds to Harrogate railway line (glance right to see the entrance to the Bramhope Tunnel). Follow the path uphill, passing to the left of a derelict red brick mill and to the right of some cottages. At the top of the hill the track bears right through the yard of Dean Grange Farm and shortly afterwards bears left again, passing a subterranean building on the right. A few yards past this fork right off the track up the bank to a stile by a gate.

Walk along near the edge of the field with a wall to your left, cross the stile in the field corner and bear right along the edge of the next field, now with the wall to your right. Bear left at the end of the field towards the wood, and when you reach it enter it through a gateway in the wall on the right. The clear path bears slightly left and then right to emerge from the wood by a step-stile. Cross the plank bridge and bear left to the tarmac access road to Oaks Farm; turn right along it, immediately keeping left at the fork, but where it bears right to drop to the farm keep straight forward on a clear track. At the end of the field ignore a track forking left uphill and keep forward through the gate, then bear left along the edge of the next field on a faint track. Cross the stile by the gate in the field corner and bear left round the edge of the next field, ignoring the gate in the next corner and turning right with the edge of the field and the wall to your left. Cross the stile in the next corner and keep forward along the right hand edge of the field to reach Scotland Lane over a stile.

Turn right along the road. In 200 yards at the next road junction turn right down the stony access road to Dean Head. Keep straight down, ignoring tracks forking left and right to houses, and at the bottom keep forward, passing to the right of Dean House, through a gate into a fenced path. Cross a beck and keep forward into a wood. The clear path keeps close to the left hand edge of the wood and leaves it by a stile. Bear left up the edge of the field to re-emerge onto the Otley Old Road over a stile. Turn left, pass High Trees Garden Centre and a layby much used by plane spotters, and in a few yards at the road junction cross the signposted stile on the right, then in a few yards another stile, and walk down the field with the wall/fence to your left.

Cross the stiles and footbridge in the bottom and head straight on, up towards Woodlands Farm. Go through a kissing-gate by a gate in the wall on the right just below the farm and follow the garden wall on your left to the corner, there going left with it to pass through another kissing-gate and pass to the right of the farmhouse to another kissing-gate and the road. Bear left up the road. In about 250 yards cross a signposted stile on the right and follow the edge of the field with a wall/fence to your right. At the end of the field turn left with the wall and 15 yards from the corner cross the step-stile in it and immediately another stile in the fence.

Walk straight across the next field towards some trees (fine views ahead and to the right). Cross the next stile and bear slightly left away from the field edge on a faint path, with Bramhope visible ahead. Cross the stile and cut the corner of the next field to a plank bridge and stile. Keep on the same line, diagonally across the next large field, to a stile in the far corner. Now follow the wall on your left (abundant nettles in summer!) soon entering an old hedged/walled way, which leads back to Old Lane in Bramhope. Turn right to return to the starting point.

BRAMHOPE TO CALEY CRAGS, POOL BANK AND ARTHINGTON BANK

WALK 19

3¾ or 7¼ miles (6 or 11½ km); Explorer 297; a mixture of tracks and field and woodland paths with superb views of Lower Wharfedale; several quite steep descents, and several busy main roads to cross. Part of the route coincides with both the Ebor Way and the Leeds-Ilkley Dales Way Link.

By bus: No. 780 Leeds-Otley (hourly, no evening or Sunday service), X84/784 Leeds-Ilkley/Skipton (half-hourly, hourly evenings and Sundays) from Leeds Central Bus Station. Alight at Bramhope Church, and keeping the church on your left walk up Church Hill to the crossroads at the top, there turning right past the Fox and Hounds along Old Lane.
By car: From the crossroads by the Fox and Hounds in the centre of Bramhope village take the road signposted to Bradford (Old Lane) and after 100 yards, opposite Old Forge Mews, turn right into the free car park (with toilets) (GR 247 433). To start the walk return to Old Lane and turn right along it.

Continue along Old Lane as far as the last house on the right. Immediately beyond this turn right along the signposted footpath. At the end of the walled section bear left and cross a stile, continuing with a broken wall to your left and passing through an old gateway en route. After going through another former gateway cross the next field diagonally right to a stile by a massive old stone gatepost, after which you follow the wall on your right to another stile, then on to the houses. Here go through the gate and follow the enclosed path to the busy A658 Bradford to Harrogate road. Cross this with great care and go left for 15 yards before turning right along a track (note the Ebor Way signpost: the Ebor Way links the Cleveland Way at Helmsley with the Dales Way at Ilkley.

Cross a stile by a gate and follow the track to its end, here crossing the stile between two gates and following the wall on the left to another stile into the wood. Follow the clear path along the left hand edge of the wood, and when you reach a cross track by a line of overhead cables turn right along it. You are now in the Danefield Estate, part of the Chevin Forest Park, owned by Leeds Metropolitan Council. In a short distance ignore a track forking left, and shortly after you pass under the power lines ignore another track forking left. When you reach a junction, go through the kissing-gate ahead and immediately take the right fork (heading towards two wooden pylons) but before you reach them bear left with the main path and follow it until you can fork right to the edge of Caley Crags, from where there is a superb view over Lower Wharfedale.

Now walk back a few yards from the edge and turn left along the first path (towards the two pylons again); by the second of them there is a fork: keep left, i.e. straight ahead, on a narrow path which drops a little and runs along some way below the edge of the escarpment. (At the fork a few yards further along it doesn't matter which path you follow.) When you reach a track, with a large gate on the right, turn left down it and follow it to the A660 Leeds to Otley road. Cross this with care and turn right to the next corner. (Buses back to Bramhope/Leeds are available from here.)

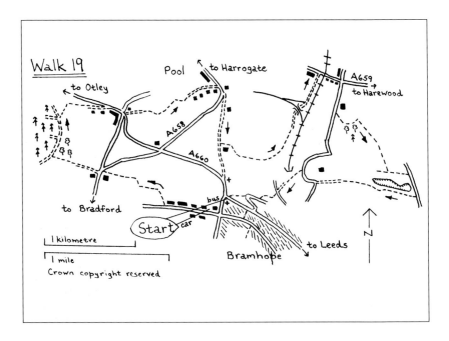

Ignore Old Pool Bank on the left, but immediately after the Bar House (site of a former toll bar) turn left along the track (signposted). Having entered woodland the track begins to descend, passes a sort of layby on the left by a rocky outcrop and curves slightly left: just before this curve look out for a narrow path forking right. This soon reaches a broader path at a T-junction: bear left here and soon emerge by some houses. Pass the right hand end of these and turn left along the back of the terrace on a path which soon bears right down into the woods. At the foot of the slope you reach a path junction. A short distance ahead and on the left there is a stile on the edge of the wood. Cross this and follow the path forward across a field.

On your right you will see an avenue of chestnut trees and the path leads into this; cross a stile and follow the avenue down to the A658 Bradford to Harrogate road once more. Having passed under the arch, look up to discover the name of the chestnut avenue: Avenue des Hirondelles. Cross the road: take care, because your view right is restricted and the traffic comes down fast, and turn right up the footway. Pass the entrance to Firs Hill Court and keep left past the post box into a descending tarmac lane, which leads to the right of a large house, then narrows and starts to climb steeply.

This is Staircase Lane, and for the shorter walk you must follow it all the way to the main road, where you can catch a bus back to Leeds, or to return to the car bear left past the 17th century Puritan chapel and fork right at Bramhope parish church up Church Hill to Bramhope Cross.

For the longer walk, climb Staircase Lane until 20 yards before the tarmac starts at Staircase House: here turn left along a track to a stile by a gate. A faint track continues half-right across the field to a gate in the far corner; ignore a kissing-gate on the right and walk down the right hand edge of the next field to another kissing-gate in the far corner, which gives access to a fenced path. Follow this to its end and another kissing-gate; now bear slightly left down a shallow valley, soon joining a clear track. Before the track goes through a gate fork right off it and follow the fence on your left to the field corner. Now walk along with a fence to the left and a row of sycamores to the right to a stile a few yards to the left of a gate, which gives access to a grassy track.

The railway to your right is the Leeds to Harrogate line, which has just emerged from the Bramhope Tunnel (look back to see the entrance). Follow the track until you reach a fork, where a track on the right leads you over a stile by a gate and through a tunnel (above was the old line to Otley). Soon you pass through a gateway and bear left down a wide unsurfaced road through another tunnel to the A659 Pool to Harewood road and turn right along it under yet another railway bridge (there is a footway on the other side and the Wharfedale Inn is a short distance to the left). Take the next minor road on the right (Creskeld Lane) and follow it until you reach a public footpath sign on the left.

Cross the stile and walk diagonally right across the field to a stile in the far corner, then follow the left hand edge of the next field to a stile in the next corner by the wood; cross this and walk along with the wood to your right until you reach a gate which leads to a fenced footpath through a narrow piece of woodland to another gate.

Now bear half-right, towards the corner of wood projecting into the field; having passed it, you will see a kissing-gate in the fence ahead. Pass through and bear very slightly left up the slope on a faint path. There is an extensive view back over Lower Wharfedale. As you get higher, you will see that you are heading for a hedge, which ends in a few yards of fencing in the middle of the field. Pass this corner and continue uphill with the fence to your right. The fence becomes a wall, which you follow up to a stone step-stile by a gate. Cross and keep uphill along the right hand edge of the field; ignore a gate on the right, and now you have a wood to your right. Follow the wall up to the corner, where there is a stile into the wood. Turn left on the path along the edge of the wood. At the motor road turn right up to the top of Arthington Bank, ignoring the entrance to Arthington Quarry on the right.

About 150 yards after the road levels out take the signposted bridleway on the right, a rather narrow and sometimes muddy path along by the quarry. Pass through a gate and keep forward, following a ditch on the left. Bramhope is visible ahead, with the Forte Crest Hotel prominent. The path becomes a track, which leads to a motor road, Creskeld Lane again. Turn right along it as far as a signposted bridleway on the left, opposite a gate in the wall on the right.

The path leads eventually to a tarmac drive: follow this up to the street and cross straight over to the continuation of the bridleway. This also leads to a tarmac drive and another street: here keep your line, diagonally right across it, to the continuation of the bridleway. Follow the path up to the next street and turn right along it. On the next rising left hand bend the bridleway forks right, with a ravine to the right, and leads back up to the A660 on the bend opposite Bramhope Parish Church. (Just before you reach the road notice the old Bramhope well and pump on the left.) From here either catch a bus back to Leeds or cross the road with great care and walk up Church Hill (notice the old milestone on the corner) to the cross, there turning right to return to your car.

Bramhope Well

74

GOLDEN ACRE TO HAREWOOD

WALK 20

8¾ miles (14 km); Explorer 297; Golden Acre, one of Leeds City Council's showpiece parks, is popular with gardeners, children who like feeding ducks, birdwatchers who like looking at them, dog-walkers, indeed anyone who enjoys walking in beautiful and well-cared for surroundings. Our walk uses field paths, tracks and short stretches of minor road to link Golden Acre to Harewood Park, another piece of fine landscape on a somewhat grander scale.

By bus: No. 780 Leeds-Otley (hourly, no evening or Sunday service), X84/784 Leeds-Ilkley/Skipton (half-hourly, hourly evenings and Sundays) from Leeds Central Bus Station to Golden Acre Park. Having got off the bus, don't cross the main road to the Park but walk back 100 yards and bear right into the car-park.
By car: Park in the main car-park for Golden Acre on the A660 Leeds to Otley road.

Walk to the Leeds end of the car-park, go down the steps and bear left to pass under the main road and enter the Park. Turn left at the T-junction and stay on the main track until you reach a broad tarmac cross-track, with the main Park entrance a short distance to the left. Turn right to the Bakery Coffee House and toilets. Having passed the café keep right at the fork and pass to the right of a bungalow.

Follow this main track along until you reach a fork: keep left and head for a wooden gate leading out of Golden Acre. Turn left up the track. You reach the road at a junction: cross straight over the first road and take the second one, half-right (King Lane). Where the wood on the left begins, cross the signposted stile and follow the path into the wood. The path keeps close to the fence on the left. Cross another stile and keep forward through the wood. Never far from the left hand edge of the wood, the path leads to another road. Turn left along it. A few yards before the next house on the right, turn right along the signposted lane (Swan Lane).

By a footpath sign the track turns sharp right towards Lineham Farm. (A proposed diversion here will move the right of way to the left hand edge of the field on the right of the track, with a kissing-gate at each end.) Pass through the wide gateway into the old farmyard and in a few yards a sign points half-right: follow the path along to a stile, then keep by the fence on the left to another stile. Walk straight across the middle of the next field to a stile just to the right of a gate on the far side. Keep forward over the next field, towards the right hand end of the farm ahead, to reach a marker post near a large solitary tree by a gate in the wall on the right.

Bear left along the remains of a track, keeping the wall to your right, to a stile by another gate ahead. Keep forward on the track for a few more yards, but where it bears right to the farm, fork left off it and make for a stile 5 yards to the right of the gate in the top corner of the field. Cross and follow the hedge/fence on the left to the next footpath sign and road.

The New Inn is a short way left along the road, but you only go left for 20 yards to the next signposted footpath on the right. Cross the stile and bear slightly left, to walk across the middle of this large field. Pass close to a power line pole and keep the same line to a stile in the hedge on the far side. Now follow the hedge on the right to the next stile, and turn left along the track. You are now on the Leeds Country Way. Follow the track as it twists and turns, eventually reaching a fork where you turn sharp right (follow the signpost and waymark). At the next T-junction turn sharp left again and climb past Stub House Farm. Over to the right is the purpose built set for YTV's "Emmerdale Farm" series.

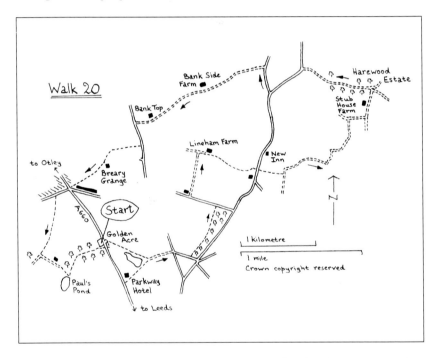

Over the brow of the hill you enter woodland. When you reach a crossing of tracks the Leeds Country Way goes right, but you take the first track on the left and join the Ebor Way. Look right through the trees for a glimpse of Harewood House. Follow the track to the next road and turn left uphill, with a lovely view right over Lower Wharfedale. Take the first minor road on the right downhill. Ignore a farm entrance on the left but take the next lane on the left, a No Through Road. When the track forks at Bank Side Farm keep straight forward, crossing a stile to the right of a barn, on a clear track. Cross another stile by a gate and now you are in an old lane. Cross another stile by a gate and continue up Bank Top Lane. Follow the track to the left of Bank Top Farm and on to the next road (automatic gate). Turn left.

Look out for a footpath sign and kissing-gate on the right. Go through the gate and follow the fence on the left through two fields and another kissing-gate to a third kissing-gate. Here bear half left over the next field to a ladder-stile to the left of a solitary tree. Keep straight forward across the next large field, passing to the left of another solitary tree and making for a stile at the right hand end of a short row of trees in the fence ahead. The stile turns out to be in a fence corner: cross it and keep down parallel to the fence on the left for about 30 yards until you have passed the left hand end of a deep ditch which crosses the field. Now bear half right, heading for the right hand corner of the gardens of the houses on the left, where you bear slightly more right towards the Shell Garage on the far side of the main road. Cross the stile and the A660 and take the No Through Road opposite (The Sycamores).

Opposite house number 8 cross the stile on the left and follow the left hand edge of the field. At the end of the third field cross a stile and now follow the edge of the wood on your right. Pass through a gateway with a redundant stile and turn left along the track (Leeds Country Way again). Pass to the right of the renovated Rushes Farm and follow the fence forward to a gate into the wood. Bear half-right, ignoring the path more sharply right parallel to the edge of the wood. Soon a path climbs an embankment on the right to Paul's Pond. Turn left along the edge of the pond, but only as far as the next corner, where you fork left again and drop to cross a plank bridge over a beck. Bear left on the waymarked path (Leeds Country Way) parallel to the edge of the wood. Pass through a wooden barrier and bear right along a broad track. It brings you to a fenced boardwalk through Breary Marsh Nature Reserve which leads back to your starting point.

THE LEEDS AND LIVERPOOL CANAL

WALK 21

The basic towpath walk is 6¼ miles (10 km), but there is so much to see on the way and there are so many interesting detours that I suggest you make a day of it! Explorers 289 and 288. I have used part of the route in Walk 22, but as this ramble from the city centre to Rodley is a Leeds classic with so much to offer both the historian and the lover of nature I felt I had to include it as a walk in its own right. In 1981 the Leeds City Council established the Museum of Leeds Trail along this route, and I am indebted to its guidebook for much of the historical information in what follows.

Buy a Day Rover and leave your car at home for this one! The walk starts at Leeds Rail Station and finishes at Rodley, from where buses 760, 670, 671 will return you to Leeds Central Bus Station and 81, 82 will take you to Horsforth and Holt Park.

On emerging from Leeds Station walk straight over the pedestrian crossing to a small white tower building with a sign saying Way Out Bishopgate, go down the steps and turn right to follow the road under the station. Turn right through the arches leading to Granary Wharf, and cross the Aire, which flows under the station, just before entering the Wharf shopping precinct. After exploring the interesting collection of shops make your way to the car park alongside and turn right along the pavement. At the end of the car park you reach the Leeds Canal Basin. Bear left to the 18th century bridge over the canal with the canal company's original office behind it, but without

Canal Milestone

crossing the bridge keep forward along the towpath. The two 19th century Italianate campaniles on the other side belong to the Tower Works.

Bridge 225G is Monk Bridge of 1886, with the city arms incorporated into its ironwork. The next impressive stone bridge with the very large arch and balustrade was built in 1846 for the Leeds and Thirsk Railway. Pass under the bridge, and just after the St.Ann's Ing Lock, on the other side of the canal, are the long low brick railway workshops with the large round-headed windows. The next concrete bridge carries the Inner Ring Road, and when you emerge from it your eye is caught by the large brick Castleton Mill of 1838 with its semi-circular stair tower

Tower Works

78

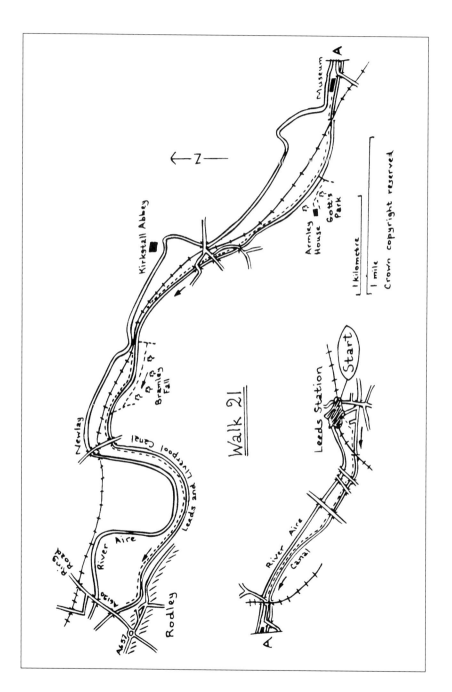

Walk 21

Museum

A

← N →

Kirkstall Abbey

Newlay

Bramley Fall

Leeds and Liverpool Canal

Ring Road

River Aire

A6120

A657

Rodley

Armley House

Gott's Park

1 Kilometre

1 mile

Crown copyright reserved

Leeds Station

Start

River Aire

Canal

A

Leeds and Thirsk Railway Bridge

Former Railway Workshops

The murals at Oddy's Locks ("Fragments from the Post-Industrial State") are by Graeme Willson (1981-84). Having passed Spring Garden Locks, the massive wall on the other side of the canal is part of the foundations of the 19th century Leeds Forge. The next very striking feature is the Leeds and Thirsk Railway viaduct built in 1846. Continuing, look out for the attractive cast-iron balustrade of the Canal Road Bridge, now on a modern concrete base. To visit Armley Mills, the Leeds Industrial Museum, which is straight ahead of you after you pass under the Canal Road Bridge, turn right immediately after the bridge through the arch and up the steps, then turn right again to cross the bridge and right again into the museum car park.

Our walk continues along the towpath. The arched stone bridge 225, giving access to the museum, dates from the 1770s. At the end of the high wall enclosing the museum turn right to the viewpoint over the River Aire: the large mill dam is conspicuous. Pass under the railway bridge, and soon two concrete bridges carry the towpath over the entrances to Power Station Wharf, where barges used to bring the coal for Kirkstall Power Station, but which is now a quiet backwater. The towpath is now quite rural, with the wooded Gott's Park across the canal.

For a detour through the Park, landscaped by Humphrey Repton, to the classical Armley House, once the residence of Benjamin Gott, the

Armley House

owner of Armley Mills, cross the next stone bridge (224) and in 20 yards turn right off the drive, in another 15 yards forking left on a clear climbing path which soon bears right and rises through the woods to a flight of steps. At the top you emerge into the open Park, now occupied by Gott's Park Golf Club, and by following the path round the edge of the wood on your right you reach two tarmac paths, either of which will take you to the house, which now serves as the clubhouse for the golf course. Notice the fine views back to the city centre and up the valley to Kirkstall Abbey and beyond. Return by the same route to the canal towpath.

When you reach a bridge preceded by a grassy space with benches and a car park, a detour to Kirkstall Abbey is possible: the route is described in Walk 22. Your walk continues along the towpath. The large building on the other side of the canal by the bridge is the former

Kirkstall Brewery, from which last century beers were carried down the canal to Goole and exported to Australia and New Zealand. Bridge 221A is the Leeds and Bradford Road Bridge, and after it look right for views of Kirkstall Abbey, the best probably being the one from Kirkstall Lock. From the three-rise Forge Locks the buildings of Kirkstall Forge, once an important iron foundry, can be seen across the railway and the river.

Here too another detour is possible through Bramley Fall, 100 acres of woodland owned by the City Council, an area once extensively quarried: it was from here that the stone came to build Kirkstall Abbey. The woodland paths while attractive are often muddy, and the drier alternative is to remain on the towpath.

If you do decide to make the detour, cross the canal by the top lock and the overflow channel by the footbridge, and ignoring the flight of steps ahead bear right along a clear path. At a fork keep left on the main path which climbs gently through the woods, and at the next fork again keep left to climb some steps to a broad cross track. Turn right along this, and walking parallel to the canal below you on the right, follow it all the way to where another broad track comes in from the left and Newlay Locks are to your right. Keep forward to the locks and re-cross the canal by the lock gate. Resume your journey along the towpath.

At the next stone road bridge (221) a detour is possible right to the 18th century Abbey Inn and the charming Newlay Bridge (see Walk 22), but your route continues along the towpath. Shortly after passing the marina the Georgian Whitecote House is seen across the canal. Just after

Rodley Barge

swing bridge 218 there is an entrance on the right into Yorkshire Water's Rodley Nature Reserve with a notice about opening times. Follow the towpath all the way to Rodley, and having passed the Rodley Barge on the other side of the canal, cross the canal by the swing bridge and turn left along Dalmeny Terrace to pass the inn and reach the main road.

Turn right for a short distance for the bus stop for buses back to Leeds (there are toilets opposite), and a little further on the other side of the road is the stop for buses to Horsforth, Cookridge and Holt Park.

KIRKSTALL ABBEY TO NEWLAY

5½ miles (9 km); Explorer 288. The walk follows almost exactly one of the suggested walks through the Kirkstall Valley Park, and is waymarked almost throughout by a blue square inside a yellow arrow. The Abbey itself, the Abbey House Museum and the Lapidarium in the abbey grounds are all worth a visit.

By bus: No. 732, 733, 734, 735, 736 Otley/Ilkley bus (frequent) from Leeds Central Bus Station to Kirkstall Abbey. Cross the main road to the carpark opposite the Abbey House Museum off Abbey Walk.
By car: Park in the Kirkstall Abbey car park opposite the Abbey House Museum off Abbey Walk (GR 259 363).

Having explored the Abbey, Museum and Lapidarium, walk towards the far side of the car park away from the museum and turn right uphill on the grass with a wood to your right. Keep straight up, to pass through a gap in the hedge ahead, cross straight over the road and up Kepstorn Rise. Keep straight over the next street, Kepstorn Close, and up the path into the wood. Bear right, pass between bollards, then bear left over the Leeds to Harrogate railway. Now keep straight forward, ignoring paths to left and right, until near the top side of the wood the path bears right, with houses over to the left. When you reach an old tarmac road leading towards the wood, cross it diagonally right and continue along the tarmac path with houses to the left and the wood to the right. When the wood ends you reach a T-junction: fork left and walk between the houses to reach Queenswood Drive through bollards.

Cross over and continue along Queenswood Road, but after 80 yards, before the next street on the left, go up a tarmac ginnel on the left which soon becomes a path through woodland and bears right with a fence to the right and the wood to the left. When the houses on the right end and you emerge into Beckett Park, keep forward along the right hand edge of the wood. There are swings and a chute down to your right should you need them. The path bears left towards Leeds Metropolitan University's Beckett Park Campus; with a university building ahead, turn left along a tarmac road.

1858 Memorial Arch

With a redbrick building 60 yards ahead, fork right on another tarmac drive following the sign to the Athletics car parking. Before you reach the athletics ground and another redbrick building, fork left between rhododendrons on a broad track, which soon leads you to an arch commemorating Queen Victoria's visit to Leeds in 1858 for the opening of the Town Hall. Pass to the right of the arch and continue forward, now on a narrow path.

Soon you are joined by another path from the left. When you reach a tall fence, go through a turnstile in it and follow the path descending

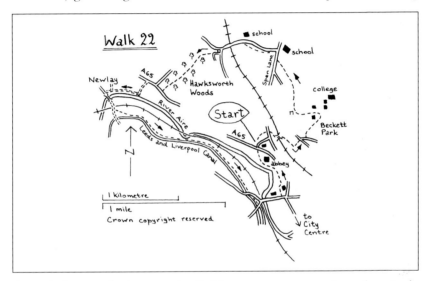

through the woods. Pass a pair of old stone gateposts and another single stone gatepost, and keep forward across the grass, to pass to the right of some trees; keep these to your left, and where they end bear right along a fence with redbrick houses beyond it. Where the fence turns left, bear slightly left to pass another old stone gatepost in the middle of the grass and reach Spen Lane through a row of trees.

Cross Spen Lane, turn right for a few yards and take the first road on the left (Butcher Hill). When you reach some playing fields on the left, a line of lampposts across the grass indicates the route of the footpath. Near the far end you pass Abbey Grange School and drop to rejoin the road. When the pavement gives out cross the road, ignore the footpath sign pointing right along the bottom of the school grounds and keep forward over the railway bridge. Re-cross the road and continue downhill. Ignore the first road on the left (although the yellow arrow points along it!), but 50 yards further on take a ginnel on the left, which leads to Cragside Close, where you bear right. The street soon bears left, and a footpath forks right off it into Hawksworth Woods (and now you are back with the yellow arrow!).

84

Having entered the wood, watch closely for the arrows. Go right at the first fork, left at the second and left at the third, cross straight over a broad cross track and at the next T-junction follow the arrow left. Oil Mill Beck is a short distance to your right. The path leads past some splendidly climbable rocks before being joined by a clear path from the left; ignore a path forking left just after this and drop to the A65. A quick, but boring way back to your starting point would be to turn left along this main road. But instead cross it (there is a helpful island a short way to the right) and turn right.

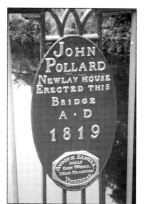

Newlay Bridge Sign

A sign soon indicates that you are entering Horsforth. Immediately after the first house on the left turn left down a stony track (bridleway sign). Cross an old mill race just before the track bears right, and now you are close to the river Aire. Just after you reach some houses you can glimpse the weir on the left at which the mill race starts. Walk forward and then turn left over the cobbled Newlay Bridge, erected in 1819 and one of the oldest iron bridges in the county. This is a delightful spot.

Now you enter the Kirkstall Valley Park. Keep forward along the road and cross the modern railway bridge (Leeds to Ilkley/Skipton lines); down on the right is the 18th century Abbey Inn. Just beyond the bridge you will see two tracks on the left: take the second of these, but in 5 yards fork right off it beside the map-board on a path which leads up to the towpath of the Leeds and Liverpool Canal. Turn left along this. At Newlay Lock you can either continue along the towpath or cross the canal and the following footbridge to walk through Bramley Fall park.

If you choose the latter, from the footbridge bear half left and cross straight over a broad track along the 'canal side walk'; in fact you walk parallel to the canal, but some distance from it, at first on an embankment, and at one point rising quite high above the canal, on a broad woodland path. Ignore two signposted right forks, but 30 yards after the second of these fork left down some steps. At the foot bear right and re-cross the canal at Forge Locks.

Abbey Inn

Turn right along the towpath. Soon Kirkstall Abbey is visible over to the left. Immediately after passing under Bridge 222 (the large building across the canal is the old Kirkstall Brewery, now accommodation for students of the Leeds Metropolitan University) bear left before the benches to the road. Go a yard or two left to the T-junction then right along Broad Lane to the traffic lights, passing the Hollybush Farm Conservation Centre, which can be visited.

At the traffic lights bear right over the Aire and walk past the Allders store. It is difficult to cross this busy road, so follow it to the traffic lights at the A65, cross it there, then walk back along the other side until you reach a gateway between black railings leading to a track with an old mill goit to one's right. At a fork bear right over the wooden footbridge, then bear left at the next fork to keep off the main road and return to the abbey.

Kirkstall Abbey

HYDE PARK TO WEST PARK, ADEL AND GOLDEN ACRE

WALK 23

3 miles (5 km) to West Park, 5 miles (8 km) to Adel, 7½ miles (12 km) to Golden Acre; Explorer 289, 297. A linear footpath route almost from the city centre to the countryside north of Leeds, largely along the valleys of Meanwood Beck and Adel Beck, a route also used by the Meanwood Valley Trail and the Leeds-Ilkley Dales Way Link. In Golden Acre Park is the Bakery Coffee House.

By bus: No. 1, 28, 55, 93, 96, 655, 755, 731, 780, 784 from the City Centre to Hyde Park.
By car: If you are intending to walk the whole route, it may be easier to park at Golden Acre on the A660 Leeds to Otley road, take the No. 780/784 bus to Hyde Park, then walk back to the car.

From the traffic lights at Hyde Park keep the Hyde Park pub on your left and walk for a few yards along Woodhouse Street, but at the end of the pub building turn left between bollards along a paved path which soon bears right and joins a cobbled lane. Pass Regent Park Terrace on the left, and at the next junction continue forward up Cliff Lane. A yard or two after passing Grosvenor Park Gardens fork left along a narrow ginnel. Keep your line across the first street you meet and continue along the ginnel to a gap-stile, where you bear left for a few yards before turning right along Grosvenor Road. Look out for a gap in the high wall on the left and the continuation of the ginnel.

At the next street (Cumberland Road) bear right to find on the left at the end the final section of ginnel leading to Woodhouse Ridge. Bear left along the ridge with the valley of Meanwood Beck to your right. Drop gently to a barrier and a junction of several paths and keep forward on the level middle path across the grass. At the far side descend a few steps, cross a track, climb a couple more steps and continue along the hedged path to Grove Lane. Cross straight over and follow the path to the next road (Monk Bridge Road).

Turn right along the footway, cross the main road at the crossing and walk along Mill Pond Lane, in a few yards forking left along a footpath. Cross a footbridge and walk along with a large building to your right. Just before the end of this turn left with the path, and when the high wooden fence on the right turns right, follow it along an enclosed path. At the end pass through the bollards and keep forward along the track. A few yards before this meets a tarmac road the main route turns right over a footbridge on a paved path (see [+] below), but for West Park keep straight ahead along the street (Hollin Drive) with houses on the left and Meanwood Park on the right.

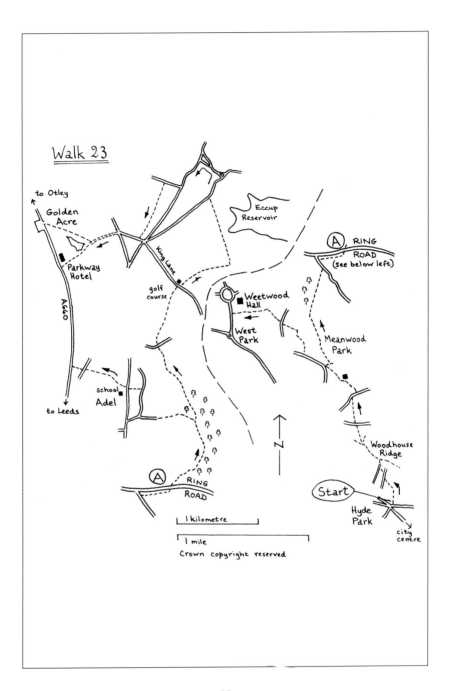

Walk 23

to Otley

Golden Acre

Eccup Reservoir

Ⓐ RING ROAD
(see below left)

Parkway Hotel

King Lane

golf course

A660

Weetwood Hall

West Park

Meanwood Park

school
Adel

to Leeds

N ↑

Ⓐ RING ROAD

Woodhouse Ridge

Start

Hyde Park

city centre

|–––––––| 1 kilometre

|–––––––––––––| 1 mile

Crown copyright reserved

Ignore the entrance into the park on the right by the pillar-box, keep right when the road forks, and soon afterwards ignore a minor road forking right. The main road begins to curve left and climb, and just after a bungalow there is a stile by a gate on the right. Cross this and walk across the grass to a car-park and bear left to another stile by a large gate. Now you have a tall iron fence to your right. Cross the stile in the far corner of the field, bear right across a stone stile and continue along the fenced ginnel, which soon turns sharply left.

When you are faced by a gate ahead cross the step-stile on the right and bear left with a garden fence to your left to a tarmac lane. Cross this and follow the continuation of the footpath with a wood to the right and a garden to the left. Shortly you cross a stile onto Weetwood Lane. Go right for a yard or two (the entrance to The Hollies, one of Leeds's delightful public parks, at its best when the rhododendrons and azaleas are in bloom, is a short distance further on) and cross to find behind a pedestrian safety barrier a cobbled ascending walled ginnel. When you reach a tarmac access road cross straight over, cross the step-stile opposite and bear left along the track with the University sports grounds to your right. At a junction of paths keep forward along a paved path with lampposts, with a fence to the right. You reach the A660 between the West Park roundabout and the Ring Road.

[+] Cross the footbridge along a paved path. Cross another footbridge, pass through a gap in the wall on the left into Meanwood Park and follow the path between the picnic tables. When the path peters out keep forward to cross a tarmac cross path, then on over the grass to pick up a clear path which bears left towards the beck. Ignore the massive clapper bridge and keep the beck to your left. Ignore several more bridges and soon you will pass through an arched gateway in a wall ahead, with a row of stone cottages up to your right. Turn left, cross the wooden bridge and turn right between stone gateposts, the beck now to your right. The path climbs a few steps and now you have an old mill goit to your left. If you crossed the next wooden footbridge on the left you would enter the Hollies, but your route keeps forward.

At the next fork keep right to re-cross the beck by a footbridge at a weir; go left for a few yards, then right down some steps. Turn left along a clear cross track, shortly passing through a kissing-gate. The beck is to your left. Follow the path until you climb a few steps onto a road: cross this and turn left along the footway. A few yards before the Ring Road turn right along a signposted tarmac drive and where this turns right through a gate keep forward along the footpath, which soon bears left to pass through a tunnel under the Ring Road. Turn right up the steps and follow the path to a stile into the woods, with Adel Beck to your right. When the path forks keep left round the outside edge of the woods, then cross a stile on the right and now the fence is on your left. Ignore a signposted bridleway on the right and at the next clear fork, keep left up the slope, and after some time the path bears right, now as a broad track through the wood. After 150 yards you reach a major fork: the main route keeps right (see [*] below), passing to the left of the Seven Arches aqueduct, but for Adel keep left.

Follow the track, at one point crossing over a cross track a few yards before you cross a disused cattle-grid, until you reach a tarmac road: bear left along it. In about 100 yards opposite an old stone house on the left turn right along a tarmac footpath with modern houses to the left and follow it round the outside edge of the houses, at first with grass then woodland to the right. At the far end of the wood fork right up a few steps and along a grit path to the next road: cross it and go right for a few yards, then fork left up the steps towards a newsagent's shop. Pass in front of it, then turn left up a tarmac footpath and follow it to the next motor road.

Adel Primary School is now to your left, but you cross the road and turn right for a few yards before entering a car-park on the left (look ahead to see part of the long causeway which gives this road its name). Take the footpath at the far end of the car-park. Pass through a gateway and walk along the right hand edge of playing fields. Another gateway leads into a ginnel. Pass through a kissing-gate and walk along the track to reach Church Lane, Adel. (The Norman parish church is a short distance to the right.) Cross diagonally left and walk along Holt Close, a no through road. At the end a ginnel leads to the A660 opposite the Texaco garage.

Seven Arches

[*] Pass to the left of Seven Arches, crossing the beck, and bearing slightly left uphill. Keeping always on the main path you will in time cross a clear cross track (notice the spring on the right) and drop to cross a shallow valley, climbing out of it by steps. Pass to the right of a small pond and bear right at the fork. Again keep to the main path. At a fork don't take the path across an open grassy area, but keep left outside its left hand edge. Pass through some dense holly bushes and keep forward over the grass to be joined by a good track from the right: bear left along this to the next road (Stair Foot Lane), passing on the way a signposted path to Adel Crag, a short detour to a rocky eminence. Cross the road and take the path opposite, ignoring a minor path forking left in a few yards. Ignore another minor path forking right a few yards before a stile into a field. Cross this and bear right along the edge of the field. Ignore a gateway in the next corner and bear left with the field boundary. Cross a stile ahead in the next corner and keep on, soon with Headingley Golf Course to your left.

Cross straight over the next motor road (King Lane), passing to the right of the white-painted Golf Farm, along a track. When the track ends keep on with the hedge to your right and the golf course to your left. Cross a stile in the next corner and keep forward, soon with a fence to your left. A few yards before the far corner of this field, cross a stile on the left and walk at right-angles to your previous line, still with a fence to your left. Cross the stile in the far corner, and now there is a wood to your right with Eccup Reservoir beyond. Over the next stile keep forward on a clear path across the middle of the large field; near the far side the path keeps to the right of a hedge, which it follows to the next stile and road. Turn right along this.

The road drops into a dip and crosses a beck: take the left fork here. At the next junction go left again, and at the next one left again, and at the next one left again, now on a rather busier road. At the next junction turn right along Black Hill Lane. At the end of the wood on the left take the signposted footpath into it. The clear path keeps close to the right hand edge of the wood (Eccup Whin). Shortly after the wood narrows there is a redundant stile: keep forward with a fence to your right, and follow it to a stile at the next motor road. Turn right along the road (King Lane again) and follow it to a T-junction: take neither of the roads here, but cross straight over and walk down the track signposted Meanwood Valley Trail. Either follow this track all the way to the A660 at the Parkway Hotel or fork right into Golden Acre Park and reach the main road through it.

Golden Acre

SUGARWELL HILL AND THE URBAN FARM

WALK 24

2½ miles (4 km); Explorer 289. Surprisingly rural so close to the city centre. Woodland and field paths, with fine views over the Meanwood Valley to Woodhouse Ridge and the city. There is a café at the Farm.

By bus: 51/52/52A/53/53A City Centre-Meanwood-Moor Allerton (frequent, but not evenings or Sundays), 751 City Centre-Meanwood-Moortown (half-hourly, not evenings or Sundays) to Meanwood Road, stop after houses on the left end and a wood begins. Walk back a short way to the houses and start the walk at [*] below.
By car: Meanwood Valley Urban Farm is signposted from Meanwood Road. Follow the signs and park in the Farm car-park.

Walk back along the Farm access road and at the turning-circle turn left. Cross Meanwood Beck and follow the path to Meanwood Road. Cross (care!) [*] and take the ascending path into the woods. At the top of the broad flight of steps turn right along the level tarmac path. At a junction keep forward on a gently descending avenue. At a major fork keep right, soon with an iron railing on your right, then turn right, to re-cross the beck by a footbridge and follow an enclosed path past Woodhouse Cricket Club to Meanwood Road. This time there is a pedestrian crossing.

Follow the cobbled path between bollards and uphill. At the top cross a stile and pass a metal barrier into a field. Walk up the right hand edge. At the top pass through a metal gate and turn right for a few yards along a fence, cross a stile in it and turn left, to follow the top edge of the field. There is a good view right to Woodhouse Ridge. Cross a stile in the top corner and keep forward. The path climbs to a stile on the left onto a road. Ignore this and turn right on a gently climbing path. Cross straight over a signposted cross path, soon reacing a high contouring path with more fine views.

At a T-junction turn right, but in a few yards fork left down a stepped path, then bear left on a clearer path at the bottom. About 30 yards after passing a stone barn fork right down a flight of broad steps. At the bottom, turning right along the tarmac path would take you back to the Farm, but keep straight on, to pass round a large gate and follow a cobbled track which soon becomes a tarmac street. At the T-junction turn right, cross the Beck yet again, cross Meanwood Road at the pedestrian crossing and turn left, then sharp right into the first street.

At a fork keep left, with a stone wall on your left, in a few yards passing round a metal barrier. By some houses on the right (Wharfedale Grove) keep right at the fork and soon the track narrows to a footpath. At a crossing of paths keep right, and in a few yards keep right again, down the steps you climbed at the start of the walk. Bus walkers who wish to visit the Farm (and car walkers returning to their cars) should

cross Meanwood Road and take the track opposite, turning right at the
turning-circle along the Farm access road.

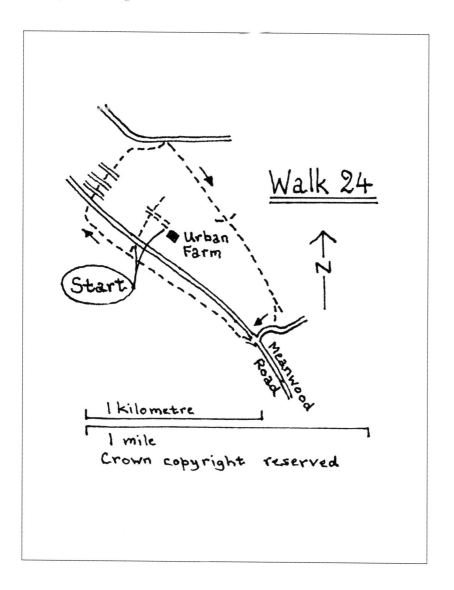

Walk 24

Urban
Farm

Start

N

Meanwood Road

1 Kilometre

1 mile
Crown copyright reserved

Record of Walks Completed

DATE	WALK	START TIME	FINISH TIME	COMMENTS				
	1. Middleton Park to Thorpe on the Hill							
	2. East and West Ardsley							
	3. Howley Park							
	4. Morley and Churwell							
	5. Farnley Park to Gildersome							
	6. Pudsey to Fulneck and Pudsey Beck							
	7. Pottering through Pudsey							
	8. Calverley circular							

Record of Walks Completed

DATE	WALK	START TIME	FINISH TIME	COMMENTS				
	9. Calverley, Farsley, Rodley and the Canal							
	10. Horsforth Circular							
	11. Horsforth to Cragg Wood and Rawdon							
	12. Rawdon Billing and Cragg Wood							
	13. Yeadon Tarn, Rawdon Billing and Spring Wood							
	14. Yeadon to Otley Chevin							
	15. Hawksworth							
	16. Guiseley to the West Chevin							

Record of Walks Completed

DATE	WALK	START TIME	FINISH TIME	COMMENTS
	17. Otley Chevin to Pool Bank and Chevin Forest Park			
	18. Bramhope to Cookridge			
	19. Bramhope to Caley Crags, Pool Bank and Arthington Bank			
	20. Golden Acre to Harewood			
	21. The Leeds and Liverpool Canal			
	22. Kirkstall Abbey to Newlay			
	23. Hyde Park to West Park, Adel and Golden Acre			
	24. Sugarwell Hill and the Urban Farm			